Praise for *Making Welcome*

"I have spent the past 40+ years in the service industry and the first thing my cousin Helen taught me when she put me behind the stick was not the proper way to stir a Martini but rather to treat your customers at the bar like you would guests in your home! With *Making Welcome: Enriching Life and Business with Hospitality*, Eddie Heintz has provided the roadmap to be successful! Whether you're just getting started or you're a seasoned veteran, you are sure to enjoy this enlightening and entertaining journey into the art of hospitality!"

—**Tony Abou-Ganim**, author of *The Modern Mixologist*

"Ten years into my professional career as a chef, Eddie Heintz took me by the hand and showed me what Hospitality was all about—caring, connecting, listening, being present, showing empathy. I will never forget the time I spent with him and the lessons he instilled in me. Eddie inspires us to find joy and love in providing hospitality just as he did with me many years ago. This book is destined to be an industry classic."

—**Tim Bodell**, director of culinary, Francis Ford Coppola Winery

"In this beautifully written and deeply personal gem of a book, Eddie shares his unique vision of hospitality. Eddie shows us that hospitality is so much more than being warm and welcoming, it is a way of life. *Making Welcome* is not just a book for hospitality professionals. This is a deeply spiritual book and may even change the way you live your life. Everyone should read it."

—**Annie Stoll**, co-founder, The Delfina Restaurant Group

"Eddie's hospitality is warm, genuine, and unparalleled. I'm so happy he's sharing his talents with a larger audience—it's such an important element of business, and his principles can easily be applied in daily life."

—**Curtis Di Fede**, chef, The Charter Oak

"I first met the author in the early '90s, the roaring decade of big and busy restaurants in San Francisco . . . I've retold this story more than a few times, 'Another very busy night, guests had tickets to the opera or the symphony, a seven o'clock curtain . . . The guests were going to be late, waiting for a car . . . then, Eddie 'steals' a car and drives them to the theater with seconds to spare' . . . this performance called for a standing ovation. That is just one story from a long and rich career in the hospitality business. For Eddie it is a reflex, intuitive, sincere service, and all of the above."

—**Richard Miyashiro**, restaurateur

"I invite you to 'open the doors' and 'connect the dots' as Eddie Heintz explores the essence of hospitality. Eddie has been observing, questioning, researching, and practicing hospitality in the 30+ years that I have known him. Thankfully, Eddie committed to put thoughts to page in this book, so we may discover our path to hospitality in our daily lives."

—**David O'Malley,** partner and head of operations, Gruppo Chiarello

"Since we met some 30 years ago, I have watched Mr. Heintz dive headfirst into many a maelstrom with little regard for his personal or professional well-being. In his obsessive need to make others feel comfortable, valued, or just plain happy, he has been overlooked, derided, and fired. And here he goes again, sticking out his neck in the world of publishing! To anyone even considering a career in the hospitality trades: read his tales of triumph, disaster, and humility. Relax, sit back, and let Eddie take you on a ride. You're welcome!"

—**Ritchie Rosen**, chef, restaurateur, and ne'er-do-well

"I have known Eddie since the early 1990s during his days in the busy restaurant scene in San Francisco through to his current hospitality role in Napa's wine country. He is the consummate host and epitomizes what it means to be a great friend, father, and hospitality professional. He says it best, 'In the hospitality industry, we learn that the guest is not always right, but they are always our guest—until they are not.' The same can be said for friends and family!"

—**Tim Hanni**, MW

"Having known Eddie for almost 30 years, I can attest to the fact that his concept of connectedness is a pillar upon which great hospitality rests. His ability to make the guest feel special under any circumstance is to be lauded. His book *Making Welcome* should be required reading at Cornell as well as by anyone who interacts with people in their business. Eddie could work in a place that served me sand and mixto tequila and I would always look forward to returning!"

—**Julio Bermejo**, beverage manager, Tommy's Mexican Restaurant; Ambassador of Tequila to North America as appointed by the National Chamber of Tequila Industry

"This is a book that goes beyond the traditional structures of how-to in hospitality, and teaches us how redefining the truth and meaning in our everyday work as hospitalitarians can be applied to create a happier, more productive, and elevated personal life as well. Refreshing, insightful, and undeniably motivating; exactly the shot of positive energy needed to reinvigorate as we navigate coming out of a pandemic."

—**Aleksa Mrdjenovich**, owner and CEO, Nova Hotels

"Immediately upon working with Eddie I felt a shared understanding of how to make people feel welcome. The kind of welcoming spirit he illustrates in *Making Welcome*. This is a spirit/environment where exceeding expectations at every turn, even in the smallest way, develops regular guests and creates/develops a culture amongst your team. This makes your guests feel hospitality is embedded in the experience. This book is an inflection of decades of experience that helped him and those of us who've been honored to work with him, truly understand what it takes to make people feel welcome in the hospitality industry."

—**Glenn Hugo**, senior winemaker, Girard Winery, Napa Valley

Making Welcome

ENRICHING LIFE AND BUSINESS WITH HOSPITALITY

EDDIE HEINTZ

RIVER GROVE
BOOKS

Published by River Grove Books
Austin, TX
www.rivergrovebooks.com

Distributed by River Grove Books

Design and composition by Greenleaf Book Group and Kim Lance
Cover design by Greenleaf Book Group and Kim Lance
Cover photograph by iStock / Getty Images Plus / Matthew Miller

Publisher's Cataloging-in-Publication data is available.

Hardcover ISBN: 978-1-63299-486-8

Paperback ISBN: 978-1-63299-484-4

eBook ISBN: 978-1-63299-485-1

First Edition

DEDICATION

I would like to dedicate this book to my two daughters,
Delia Virginia Rogers and Lucia Esperanza Adrian Heintz,
who taught me everything I needed to know in life.

Contents

TRUST

The Trailhead

I AM A LUCKY MAN. I grew up in a small town of around five thousand people in the Midwest during the '60s and '70s. Nevada, Iowa, was a town right out of *Andy Griffith* or *Leave It to Beaver*. My parents would always leave their front door open or unlocked for visitors who would enter without knocking. Car keys never left the ignition. As children, we left our bikes in the front yard at sunset and picked them back up the next morning after breakfast for further adventures.

Growing up in a small town had its advantages for me. In Nevada (pronounced Ne-vay-da, with a long A, not like the state Nevada) everyone knew you, and no one interfered in your life. I had the feeling that we looked out for each other, but for the most part, we minded our own business. I feel that this upbringing helped form the strong feelings I have around hospitality.

My parents were always trying to help where they could, volunteering their time or just being there for a neighbor. They were involved and connected to the community and family. The Heintz clan was imposing in size when the extended family was complete, and my grandmother Minnie was the matriarch. She had brunch for her kids and grandkids after church each Sunday. We always arrived at the smell of coffee and "loose meat" hamburgers in the pot. We grandkids would then flop down and watch *The Three Stooges*, *Popeye*, and other cartoons, play a game of hide the thimble, or go outside for a game of kickball. A plaque that my dad got for my mom on her birthday states, "Love is sharing my life with you." It is one of my most treasured possessions.

In high school, I grew to like photography (observing) and writing (describing). I played bass in a couple of bands but never played (or practiced) enough to be taken seriously. The three chords of punk rock were made for my abilities, and I hit them hard in both Positive Abuse and Toys, the only two bands I played in. I guess you could say, in retrospect, that I had three main strengths: I was flexible and adaptable, but mostly, I was *game*. I would try most things once. I learned to skydive and scuba dive. I learned to bartend (useful income for the rest of my life). I got my degree in biology (my first love), and I rode motorcycles (my second love). I could perform all of these duties adequately but excelled only at riding motorcycles, due to the amount of time in the saddle.

Through my life, the common thread of "who I really am" has been helping to make people feel welcome and heard. I could say that this is how I was raised, but it may have more to do with nature than with nurture. I seem to be more passionate about unique connections. I would spend a lot of time observing, learning, and experiencing the complexities of human connection. These complexities always fascinated me, and until recently, I was not clear why.

Over time I had collected in my active mind a myriad of disciplines and information that I felt was relevant for increasing the hospitality experience around me. My collections of thoughts made sense to me, but I wasn't sure how I could best relay this information to anyone else without locking them in a room with me for hours. I pretty much kept the ideas that were formulating from my readings and research to myself. I would try various ideas on for size to see what worked and what didn't, in the laboratory of restaurants in San Francisco, Hawaii, and Napa. Eventually what I had learned got to be too much to keep in, and I started getting some of these thoughts and teachings on paper and sharing them with my coworkers.

A while back, a friend, Katie McKay, suggested I take a little quiz. It was based on a book called *StrengthsFinder* by Tom Rath. In this quiz, you are asked a series of questions in quick succession to see where your strengths lie. There is a substantially long list of strengths that are possible. They range from Achiever to Strategic, and Arranger to Maximizer, and Harmony to Competitive. I took the test, and the light came on in a big way. The results I got from the test made perfect sense—of me. It explained what I had been doing my whole life and most importantly *why*.

My #1 strength is Connectedness. Surprise! I have always looked for connections among people and seemingly random things. (You may pick up on this early on.) I love connecting the dots. It doesn't matter if it is a 1:1 connection with a total stranger, finding commonality between two totally different concepts, or finding connectedness within a group. This is where I get my joy, and this is what this book is about.

Once you take the test, a personalized sheet is emailed to you with the results and descriptions of each strength. Here is what mine said about Connectedness, my #1 strength: "People who are especially talented in the Connectedness theme have faith in links between all things. They believe there are few coincidences and that almost any event has a reason." Nailed it! That's my religion, my spirituality, my joie de vivre! I am fascinated with certain ideas and philosophies that affect humans and all creatures around the world. I like to link these ideas for a higher understanding. I am optimistic, and I shy away from negativity; I get uncomfortable when people are blaming others. The only people I consistently trash talk are close friends, an odd form of affection. This questionnaire and printout were better than a crystal ball, tarot cards, or tea leaves for me. The experience was also easier on the wallet than a session with a professional. My heart sang when I read that "fortifying the bonds between yourself, the people you know, or even those you will never meet gives your life special meaning." It is no wonder I receive great joy in my work from pleasing total strangers.

The other strengths that were identified are, in order of appearance: Relater: "Deep satisfaction in working hard." *Yep! I love my work.*

Developer: "Spot the signs of each small improvement and derive satisfaction from these improvements." *These incremental improvements fuel my optimism.*

Arranger: "Figure out how all of the pieces and resources can be arranged for maximum productivity." *I love to organize things. My mother was the same. I used to say that she had files on where her files were. Or as my friend Don Wetherell says, "Systems will set you free."*

Includer: "Without hesitation, you sometimes dive into conversations with old friends, new acquaintances, or even total strangers . . . You have tender feelings for all sorts of people." *I feel that this should have been higher on the list; I am always looking to rope in the outsider in a group and make new connections.*

The joy, curiosity, and passion around my love of practicing hospitality—along with the need to connect the dots—has taken me on a journey of discovery in my life. I have spent the last thirty-plus years exploring philosophies and ideas and connecting seemingly unrelated concepts that I feel have a play in hospitality. Throughout this process, I feel blessed to uncover and discover who I really am (for now), and I feel fortunate to be able to ply my trade and quench my thirst for *how* and *why.*

This is a book that will help you to uncover the how and why, also the what and when (the who is you). My intention was to take the reader on a meandering path, rich with scenic overlooks and thoughtful moments. I have loosely organized the information into seven chapters. In chapter 1, "What Is Hospitality Anyway?", we get right into defining what hospitality means, or more accurately what it is not. By defining the word and intent around the word, we can proceed and expand on its depth and riches.

Everyone that builds and creates needs specialized tools of the trade. Chapter 2, "The Hospitality Tool Chest," helps us to stock up on practices that will aid us in making people feel welcome. These practices are not easy, but in time we gain strength, and the rewards are long term.

Chapter 3, "The Spirit behind Hospitality," goes deeper yet. With the help of Eckhart Tolle we discover how hospitality can relieve us of our burdens that keep us from truly connecting with each other.

In "The Culture of Hospitality," chapter 4, we are able to pick up a common thread throughout varying cultures. I am still astounded that so many "tribes" isolated from each other have still come to a common philosophy. There must be some truth here.

In chapter 5, "Styles of Hospitality," we take a closer look at perception. There is no single fix for everything; it requires observation, flexibility, and courage to stay in the game until you find what works.

Which gets us to chapter 6, "Everyday Hospitality." Multiple opportunities present themselves to us every day. Each day we have a choice of continuing on in relative isolation or taking up the challenge and accepting the gift that has been presented. I vote for picking up the gift and enriching our lives.

Finally we get to "The Bookend," chapter 7. It is not really the end, but a nicely tied bow that wraps around a valuable gift. Within this gift is empathy, community, heart, and inspiration.

Every day, there is great hospitality being practiced all over the world, and this is changing and evolving as the world changes. As these changes progress, it is sometimes easy to lose our way, our focus. Under stress and with endless distractions we can forget about core concepts like kindness and being hospitable to others. Empathy can go by the wayside when it is needed most.

These writings are not intended to be the end-all or how-to around the subject of hospitality. They are merely a sampling of my journey and what has been exposed by the various stones I have lifted. It is one path, a path that has universal applications for me and for many others. I am no more an expert than the rest of you reading this. I have connected the dots in the way that I see them, and I feel that I have a story to tell. If John Lennon and others are correct and "love is all there is," then I believe that being connected to those around us is the great highway to receiving and giving that love. And what better way to do that than through great hospitality? What follows in these pages has been my hospitality quest; please join me on this noble journey.

"There is no new knowledge,
it already exists in the universe."

—STEPHEN RICHARDS

CHAPTER 1

What Is Hospitality Anyway?

Business, like life, is about how you make people feel.
It's that simple and that hard.

—DANNY MEYER

WHEN I THINK about *Hospitality*, it conjures up flashes of experiences that are very exciting to me. These experiences can be intense, memorable, and sometimes shameful. Hospitality has been an important part of my life for decades. It gets me up in the morning, excited for the day. It may sound geeky, but it gives me a buzz. Its importance in my life has not always been clear to me, however. I knew that I enjoyed making guests happy when they visited the restaurants that I served in or managed. But I never truly questioned why I liked it; I simply knew that I enjoyed it. Maybe that was enough.

As I looked more deeply into hospitality and how it is defined, I found it to be elusive. The concept can be hard to put into words—or at least consistent words. When I asked people—especially those in the industry—what hospitality meant to them, I got a multitude of answers, such as, "It's getting people what they want"; "It's being kind to people that you are hosting, helping make them happy"; and "It means that you are in the service industry."

Each of us has our idea of what hospitality means, and we all have fond memories of a time when we had an epic experience at a hotel, restaurant, or in someone's home. We can also have unfavorable experiences, ones that just aren't fun. And people may have vastly different perceptions of the same experience. Perhaps to one person, the staff at an event seemed to be merely going through the motions. Maybe the staff or host didn't seem into it or was too rushed. Maybe the experience came off as dry or boring. To another person it might have been an epic evening that they will remember fondly, an experience to share for years to come.

The question we must ask ourselves is why are there vastly different perceptions of the same event? Why were some expectations for you not met, while your companion's expectations may have been exceeded? What made the perceptual difference? You were both at the same event.

A few years back, I went to the Hospitality Symposium, a conference held in Wine Country. Its attendees were primarily people from hotels, restaurants, wineries, and concierge services. There was also at least one person representing a limo company. As I perused the program for the day, I realized that the subject matter for this "hospitality symposium" was all over the board. Some subjects had more to do with food-handling procedures or making better profit. At one point in the afternoon, a speaker went over the procedures that could keep a restaurant out of trouble with the Health Department. I asked myself, "What do food-handling procedures have to do with hospitality?" I considered food-handling procedures more of a sanitation and processes issue. I felt that this information was out of place at the symposium, and I was disappointed. I also felt I was wasting my time and money, but when I scanned the room, everyone else seemed to be OK with the subject. As the speaker continued with her presentation, she made a confusing statement about the restaurant, winery, and hospitality businesses. I raised my hand and asked her what she meant by hospitality business, as I had always considered restaurants and wineries as part of the hospitality business as well. She paused, thought for a moment, and replied, "I guess I meant hotels."

It was not the first time I had experienced something like this. I once had an interview with the director of hospitality for a company that had several properties. My resume told my story of managing several high-profile restaurants in the Bay Area and Hawaii. She asked, "And what makes you want to get into the hospitality industry?" I was taken aback! I had to ask her what she considered to be the hospitality industry. She said that the hospitality industry consisted of wineries and hotels. I suggested that we in the restaurant industry and culinary arts considered ourselves in the hospitality industry too. She blushed a deep red and said that she had not considered that before. Hmm. She was the *director* of *hospitality* for a company with multiple properties and at least one restaurant. What kind of directing in the arena of hospitality was going on here?

I began to understand that we have a problem with the word "hospitality." Its definition is at the very least fuzzy, and at the extreme, it has no clear meaning across a wide spectrum of people. It seems to get bandied around like a shuttlecock in a storm, then plucked down and used as a blanket term to convey a more precise meaning. In our industry, it seems to mean whatever the individual wants it to mean at any given time. I have a problem with that. As a manager of people, I have experienced that if you choose to say that everyone is responsible for a given task, it usually turns out that no one is responsible for getting that task done. For me, this philosophy translates to the word "hospitality" as well. The word gets airplay, but there is rarely a clear definition among multiple people. Because everyone defines it differently, it has become diluted, or at the very least, only potent in pockets of true understanding.

If we do a deeper dive and break hospitality down, the root derives from the Latin word *hospes*, meaning *host, guest,* or *stranger*. The word "hospes" is formed from *hostis*, which means *stranger* or *enemy*, the latter being where the word "hostile" comes from. Hospes is thus the root for the English word host (where the p was dropped for convenience of pronunciation). Hospitality, hospital, hospice, hostel, and hotel all have the same root. We could say that hospitality is derived from *hosting strangers as guests*. Even enemies can be treated like royalty if we invoke the openness of Southern hospitality or the codes of many historical and cultural beliefs.

If we look up the definition in the dictionary, we see that it can mean several things:

A noun: *the friendly and generous reception and entertainment of guests, visitors, or strangers.*

Or an adjective: *relating to or denoting the business of housing or entertaining visitors, "the hospitality industry."*

Chevalier Louis de Jaucourt describes hospitality in *Encyclopédie* as "the virtue of a great soul that cares for the whole universe through the ties of humanity." Connectedness! Could this be the root of hospitality? No one is a stranger when practicing hospitality. We are all connected.

So how shall *we* choose to define hospitality? Is it welcoming strangers into our business or home? Is it the hotel, restaurant, or winery business, or all three? Is it putting large spreads of wonderful food out for your friends or family? Can it be as simple as opening a door for someone or giving a stranger a smile? Is it supplying an umbrella to walk a friend to the car in the rain? Are acts of hospitality and manners the same thing? Can I take a picture of hospitality? Is there hospitality in art or music? How about getting an Uber for a friend who has had too much to drink and then having someone drop your friend's car off in front of their house the next morning? Am I exhibiting hospitality or just being kind? There are so many questions. Let's sort this out.

When the word "hospitality" is used in a sentence, it can take on the form of a noun, as in "She treated me with great hospitality" or an adjective, as in "I am in the hospitality industry." Inside hospitality, you will find caring, empathizing, reaching out, catching, reading, smiling, nodding, winking, joking, laughing, rewarding, pleasing, recovering, saving, cajoling, and connecting. It's the fluff and fold that we do with those around us. For these reasons, I find that at its essence, hospitality behaves more like a verb than a noun. It's the "easily done," the "graceful dance." It says I care about you, and I am paying attention to how you receive our intentions. It's the wrapping paper around the gift(s).

Is great service at a restaurant or hardware store the same thing as receiving great hospitality? I was assisted and I walked out with what I came for—I'm happy. If service and hospitality are the same things, then why are there two different words to describe the experience? I am a big believer in using the right word in any situation whenever possible. I don't believe the words "service" and "hospitality" are interchangeable. I believe there is a difference between great service and great hospitality just as there is a difference between a kiss on the cheek and one of passion. Many of the books I have read on this subject over the years refer to "a great experience" as "good customer service." The random use of service and hospitality can be confusing for many, including me.

In his book *Setting the Table*, Danny Meyer, a New York restaurateur, clears things up a bit and gets us closer to an agreement on what hospitality means. He tells us that service is what happens to us, it's the delivery of a product, it is what is physically performed. It is getting your soup spoon *before* your soup arrives; it is getting the entree that you ordered *exactly* as you ordered it. It's also hanging an "Out of Service" sign on a soda machine that is not working.

Meyer tells us that hospitality is *how* the delivery of a product makes us *feel*. It's about the demeanor, conduct, poise, attitude, and disposition of the person delivering the hospitality. He ties emotion to hospitality, not to service. If we accept his definition, we could say that an effort to make someone feel great could be called guest hospitality and not customer service. Customer service is what happens *to* us, and hospitality is how we *feel* about it. I feel that in business and in life, if we focus solely on customer service, then we are only experiencing a part of the whole—the what—and not the how, and showing no interest in the why.

We could say that the timely delivery of a dish prepared perfectly with good ingredients would be considered good service. On the other hand, if the dish was arranged and presented artfully with a specific guest in mind, could that be considered great hospitality? The chef, baker, or host are certainly plying their trade, taking pride in their work. Perhaps this scenario is motivation dependent. I'm sure that the preparer would like you to return, so making his plates presentable makes sense. But could a personalized effort toward an individual be motivated by hospitality? I think yes. If she made a specific plate for a unique guest, she has put emotion onto the plate through intent.

Some may think that this is stretching the point, but it gives us another avenue to explore. There is a reason that ancient Hawaiians would only let certain members of the community pound the poi, the sustenance for the village. Only people of pure spirit could pound poi;

they did not want bad energy going into the food they were going to put into their bodies. If the preparers were thinking bad thoughts, the Hawaiians believed that this negative energy would be transferred to the food that they would eat and therefore to the consumer. These selected individuals would prepare themselves to project positive *mana* while preparing the feast.

Often it seems that hospitality is the ether in the room, it's the invisible, the indescribable feeling that has no words. Or perhaps, more accurately, it may take volumes of words to describe. It's an energy that produces a magical event. We've all felt it, but can we name it beyond how wonderful the experience was, based on the description of its components? The likely phrase that comes to mind around these experiences is, "You had to have been there; I can't explain it." It often *is* unexplainable because we have no words for it in our language.

When wonderful, connected experiences happen at a social event, or at the dinner table, it's an emotional experience. I would wager that when you relive this experience, you realize that there was energy in the air, it was about connectedness, it was about saying yes! Saying yes to a moment, enjoying the moment by being present in that moment and paying attention to what was happening in that moment. No past, future, or other interference, only the connection that was happening in the now.

Let's imagine for a moment that you have an uncle David, and he called you to let you know that he was traveling back for a visit next month. It has been a decade since he has visited you and his hometown. You also remembered that Uncle David loved gnocchi. His favorite gnocchi came from Luigi's, a family-owned restaurant in town that has been serving your family for three generations. The idea occurs to you that since he is coming to town, you should make reservations at Luigi's because you know he will love it. But then another thought creeps in.

Instead of going out to dinner at Luigi's restaurant, why don't you attempt to make his favorite dish for him in your home? Isn't it always more personal to entertain at home?

You decide to call the restaurant and ask if you could get the recipe. Of course, they are happy to share it with you (great hospitality). You will do your best to make it identical to how they make it. You even do a few practice runs. It's not perfect, but you put your heart into it.

The day finally arrives and Uncle David walks through the threshold of your home. You are excited to see him and nervously excited for your surprise. You had already set the stage by putting on Bix Beiderbecke—his favorite jazz musician—and your spouse has deployed the martini shaker into service. Finally the moment arrives, and after everyone is seated at the table, you come out of the kitchen and present the platter of gnocchi. He recognizes the dish immediately and beams. You know that it's not exactly the *same* dish, and technically it may not be as good. But do you think that he would have had the same reaction if you had purchased it from the restaurant, or the same warmth of the family home if he had eaten it in the restaurant? My guess is that he will love the experience even more, knowing that it came from your hands. You've shown Uncle David great hospitality, and he is delighted—hospitality in both directions.

In this scenario, you have gone out of your way to make something that a specific person might enjoy. You could have made something more in your comfort zone, a dish that all guests at your house have raved about, but that would have been playing it safe and would have lacked the personal intent. It would have been more about you. Instead, you chose not to take the easy path. Your sole purpose was to please him, and you took the risk to do it. If he lives up to his "favorite uncle" status, he would have loved it no matter how it turned out because it came from you.

Danny Meyer kicked this connection concept up a notch when he popularized the phrase "enlightened hospitality." He felt that the circle was not complete. Hospitality should not be a monologue; it should be a dialogue. He suggested that we should pay attention to *how* our hospitality makes other people feel. He also dusted off the term "hospitalitarian" and breathed it into life by defining that a hospitalitarian is someone who practices this art day in and day out and actually feels rewarded by it. He even defined five core emotional skills that are essential for great hospitality:

1. Optimistic warmth: genuine kindness, thoughtfulness, and a sense that "we will find a way"

2. Intelligence: not just smarts but rather an insatiable curiosity to learn for the sake of learning

3. Work ethic: a natural tendency to do something as well as it can possibly be done

4. Empathy: an awareness of, care for, and connection to how others feel and how your actions make them feel

5. Self-awareness and integrity: an understanding of what makes you tick and a natural inclination to be accountable for doing the right thing with honesty and superb judgment

As a way of summarizing this concept, Danny Meyer believes that the most important skill a hospitalitarian possesses is a compelling desire to make others feel welcome and comfortable. Most importantly, the hospitalitarian derives pleasure from the experience of treating people well. While performing these acts of kindness with connection on occasion is certainly within the abilities of most people, the ability to maintain a connection with those in front of us all day long, year in and year out, requires a much higher commitment.[1]

In the gnocchi and Uncle David scenario, you exhibited the skills that Danny Meyer described. You displayed optimistic warmth; you knew you could pull this off because you cared deeply. You were curious and did the research; you displayed work ethic by making a few trial runs. And finally, you knew what you wanted to do and you did it; you had integrity.

You may have been anxious to see how he would react when you walked your dish to the table, but you delivered the platter of gnocchi with a proud smile. "My favorite gnocchi!" he declared. "This takes me back to my childhood at Luigi's. I didn't know you knew how to make it." You let him know that you got the recipe from the restaurant and wanted to give it a try for his visit. It has made your connection with him stronger, which opened up many conversations about family and the things you did together when you were growing up. This could be considered a great act of hospitality; you thought ahead, put yourself in his shoes, and did your best at delighting someone you care about. Most importantly, you were witnessing his delight and were able to walk with him down memory lane because the two of you were in tune with each other. You were connected.

This connection is easier with people we have known for some time. We have history to fall back on, and we learn the likes and dislikes of those we care about. But what about strangers? How can we implement enlightened hospitality to care for people we have never met? All of us have an idea of what it is to be hospitable—that is, if we have an interest. For instance, at a dinner party, you may take extra time to introduce guests to one another so that they can have a better time connecting. You could also arrange for passed appetizers at a house party so that the guests have something to soak up the drinks without stepping away from the conversation. For businesses, perhaps offering complimentary valet parking could be considered hospitable so the guests don't spend their time driving around looking for a place to park. This adds the advantage of helping to keep everyone on time for their reservation (restaurant wins). These could be examples of hospitality with the guest's interest at heart.

But perhaps this is merely your idea of what your friends and guests may want. It's projecting what you want them to have. Where do our needs end and the guest's or stranger's needs begin?

Many of us establish systems that we feel will work for most people. It has been my experience, however, that this is as far as some businesses and humans go, merely giving someone what we think that they want, whether it be a greeting, service, or an amenity. Deeper insight and listening may come later but not in the beginning. If the guest doesn't like what we thought they wanted, we may make adjustments, but doing so may not come naturally or seem fluid, *and* you will need to ask. We make a plan and we stick to it. To deviate can cause inconsistency, which is bad, right?

In the diving community, there is a phrase, "Plan the dive, dive the plan." When you are restricted by how much oxygen you have in the tank and need to calculate depths, this is a good idea, but does this regimen benefit hospitality? In restaurants where I have worked, we decided how our guests would be greeted, what we were going to offer them, and how and when they would receive it. Then we would go about our business and make adjustments when necessary. The key word here is "necessary." We were going through a process, and often we were "processing" our guests. There was often no effort to individualize the experience—the variety of choices on the menu and wine list did that, right? Most often it was a sense of "here is who I am" or "who we are," and "this is what we offer."

I feel that if you have a desire to be *most* successful, you need to be flexible. I now view the operational plan as a basic skeletal structure.

It is our job to pay attention to our guests and each other, identifying and seizing the opportunities as they arise, fleshing them out moment by moment.

I would like to take Danny Meyer's concept and explore the who, how, when, where, and why. Moving forward, the only hospitality that we will be concerned with is what Danny Meyer coined enlightened hospitality. We will call it simply hospitality. It is kind of like organic farming. Many people across the country make organic food but don't label it as such. They feel that organic should be the standard—the way everyone should grow vegetables, fruit, and grain, and raise animals. It is nothing to brag about—it is the base, the starting point. Pesticides and other harmful chemicals should never have been introduced to begin with. I like this attitude, and that is how I feel about hospitality; it should always be enlightening.

By now you have surmised I am quite passionate about the injection of hospitality in life and business. I have more passion around this than I have about the other aspects of our industry. At the risk of angering many of my chef, financial, and management friends, I have less interest in the food, the wine, the architecture, the flatware, the plates, the glasses, or even the beer list (which is a close second) than I have with how the staff interacts with the guests. To me, everything else is a stage setting, items that we need to create the ambiance, set the tone, the atmosphere—to silently tell the guests who we are.

To express another point of view, if we did not have great passion created by culinary artists, the great chef-owners, and entrepreneurs, many restaurants would not exist today. Why would people come to a place that did not have a great product, ambiance, and knowledgeable staff? You cannot eat or drink hospitality. I do not want to detract from the skills and efforts that bring us amazing, consistent meals each visit. Nor do I want to detract from the beautiful designs and artisan accoutrements that make enjoying the meal even more memorable. I especially want to pay tribute to the efforts of a knowledgeable staff. This also goes for the hosting at home. Opening your home and serving a warm meal made by hand is no small feat, including for the working mother of three boys who had dinner on the table at five thirty every night while I was growing up. I do believe, however, that great food and beauty alone will fall short of fulfilling the full potential and soulfulness of the home or restaurant. It may be the brains and body, but the soul belongs to the greater guest experience. I subscribe to the belief that the quality of food and ambiance can get the guest in the door, but hospitality is what brings them back again and again.

For me, it's not about carrying the best wine or featuring the best ingredients (of course we do, because we care). It's not about the perfect tables or chairs (unless it is to make our guests more comfortable). It's about the connections that we make with our guests each night. That's right, our guests. We don't have customers; we invite people, our guests, into "our home" every night for an enjoyable experience.

This is the passion that drives me and other like-minded people as we get up each morning (or afternoon). This passion carries us through our day, connecting with people while getting our morning coffee, buying groceries, conversing with the bank teller, and eventually, heading to work our shifts as waiters, managers, bartenders, sommeliers, baristas, barbacks, food runners, and bussers. All it takes is a sincere effort, a nod, a smile, and a hello attached to a name. These are all forms of simple recognition that we enjoy and crave.

One way to express hospitality in words comes from Sally Srok, principal of Inner Compass Consulting. Sally and I have been good friends for years. I like the way she puts it when she says, "Hospitality says, 'I care.' It is a spirit of welcoming, kindness, and the love of making people happy. It is a sense of authenticity; it's a perspective that comes from a genuine place." We have all experienced making a difference in someone's day. Making a difference can be a tough target to hit. It requires attention to details, thinking outside the box, thinking about what would blow these people away—or more accurately, what needs to happen right *now*.

One evening two ladies were dining with us at Boulevard in San Francisco. They were going to see a play after their early dinner. I began getting a little nervous because the ladies seemed to be in no hurry, and I knew that they were cutting it close. I also knew that if they were late for the play, they would not be able to attend the first act and would not be seated until the second act. I asked our host to call a cab with the idea that I would have one waiting to expedite matters. The host informed me that she had not been able to get a cab all evening because an event down the street was causing traffic problems. This was not good. I went out front hoping to hail a cab that was dropping someone else off, but I didn't see one. The ladies met me outside and began to worry with me. Just then, I recognized one of the guests who was getting ready to valet her car. I went up to her and asked if I could borrow her car. I told her I needed to get these ladies to the theater in the next few minutes. She said that she had a back seat full of wine—she worked for a distributor—and we would need to move it out first. We didn't have time, so I asked the ladies if they minded cramming into the bucket seat up front. After a harrowing ride through a few shortcut alleys, we finally pulled up to the theater with two minutes to spare. Thankfully, I knew the city well, and I am sure that it was a car ride they will never forget. Nor will they forget the restaurant that made it happen.

There are times when people or situations are challenging. I feel that any of us can overcome these challenging situations as long as you have the desire and are committed to making a concerted effort. This is where adaptability and not giving up come in. Whether your path is one of a warrior, adventurer, or journeyman, when seeking to make someone's day or turn a negative experience around, hospitalitarians quickly learn to adapt and figure out a path to give each individual a great experience.

Hospitality is not a dynamic force to be reckoned with; it is an open invitation. It does not need to be applied to guests; it is presented to them as an open door. If they eagerly walk through that door, it's time to play. If they seem to want minimum contact, a good hospitalitarian will pick up on that and find a way to deliver everything the guest needs with minimum conversation or interruption. In restaurants, we call this style silent service. Outside the restaurant, it is called giving someone space.

It is important to note that it is called silent *service*, not silent *hospitality*. All of the points of service are still happening, crisply performed, with barely a word being spoken: great hospitality. Giving guests what they need and leaving them to it may be the best hospitality in some situations. Be there if they need anything, but your occasional presence is enough. In this case, the "dialogue" is silence, and it is understood by both parties.

Hospitality is a universal method that helps return us to who we really are. It can also make your day. It costs nothing and pays huge dividends for ourselves and for those around us.

These waters that we are wading in can appear to be quite muddy. Many human interactions lack true clarity, and they can be murky and complicated no matter the effort. Let's attempt to clear the waters, stock our hospitality tool chests, and gain perspective by gathering the hospitality-enriching threads left by those who came before us.

CHAPTER 2

The Hospitality Tool Chest

You can't tell people anything,
you've got to show 'em.

—BRUCE SPRINGSTEEN[1]

N O MATTER HOW MURKY or complicated things.get, a true hospitalitarian will make hospitality look easy. It doesn't matter if you are a law firm receptionist, a county clerk, a personal assistant, or just want to make your relationship better; if you are a true hospitalitarian, you will make the effort to connect with those across from you. Grace and discipline are required to perform well. It can appear to be a graceful dance, and with desire and a little practice, you can dance with the best of them. Hospitalitarians are everywhere among us. This graceful dance happens each day with simple actions such as opening a door for someone, sharing a kind smile, offering a cup of coffee, or giving a stranded person gas, food, or money to get home. If we are aware and sincerely look out for each other, our graceful actions and interactions will benefit others and enrich our lives. These exercises in hospitality can also be the beginning of the clarity in the murkiness. The clarity comes through recognizing the potential gifts that others present as they appear before us, and through viewing these gifts as opportunities. You will find joy in embracing these opportunities as they arise.

In my earlier days as a young manager, I had no idea what I was doing. Nor did many around me; we were winging it. We were given financial goals, knew our opening and closing duties, had been briefed on the menu, and knew what needed to be done during the shift. But when it came to *how* to do it, we were in free-form. We observed how managers performed. We saw what worked, and if we were paying attention, we also saw what didn't work. It was a little like parenting; we had to determine if we would parent as our parents did or if we would choose what worked best and discard the rest. The idea was to not make the same mistakes as our predecessors and to find the best path forward.

At that time, I was not aware—before the internet made research easy—that there was potential for education around being a manager. I had little training, and I had not gone to business or hospitality school. I thought that managing was based on what I had learned in the school of experience. Thankfully, as it turned out, there were many good leaders; people with certain skill sets seemed to rise to that position. I did learn through observation.

Eventually I found a few books that enhanced my skill set. One of them was *The One Minute Manager* by Kenneth Blanchard. I was amazed to discover that I could learn from a book how to manage people better. I read more management books and began to devise my personal style. I found support with fresh ideas in these books, but I was still winging it.

In fact, when I moved from San Francisco to Hawaii in 1999, the *SF Weekly* had a little blurb about my leaving, written under the pen name Harry Coverte, that stated, "Eddie Heintz, the last of the seat-of-your-pants-front-of-the-house managers, is saying 'Mahalo' and jetting off to the Big Island. (Seems they have restaurants there, too.)"[2] Unless a manager went to Cornell or another school that taught such things, we were all flying by the seat of our pants, it was true. But the observant managers had watched and learned, passing along the art of connection, warmth, and great hospitality. We were a tribe, and we took care of each other. In San Francisco during the '80s and '90s, anytime any of our tribe came in from another restaurant, we treated them like royalty. We knew that they had worked hard to get a day off, and we were honored that they would spend that valuable time in our humble establishment. We were happy to see them and proud to show them what we could do.

When hospitality is experienced in its true essence, there is always a strong connection happening, a dialogue. It seems to me that when I feel that connection in its strongest form, my senses narrow, and there is no awareness of anything going on around me except my focused attention on that moment. I can get lost in it. At other times, I find myself performing in a more superficial state. When hospitality is not practiced deeply, it can sometimes feel like a skimming experience. It is easier to skim over the surface of the party or event instead of diving deeper due to time constraints, workload, exhaustion, other priorities, or—gasp!—lack of interest. For me, these less potent hospitality experiences can be somewhat rewarding, especially when hosting 50–150 people enjoying a great experience, but it seems to feel more like work than play. The time does not fly by as quickly. When I find myself in this situation, I will often catch myself standing alone in the middle of a room for moments at a time, looking at nothing in particular and thinking about the things that I need to do in the future or something that has happened in the past. These thoughts do not pertain to that moment, and they are distracting. It's kind of like going to a concert and sorting out your to-do list for the next day with a hundred decibels of rock and roll thundering all around you; you're detached and uninvolved in a potentially great experience.

My best memories are when the deeper connections are made, those moments when nothing else exists in the room but you and the person or people in front of you. You can experience this sense of engagement either as the host or a guest. You catch yourself excited about that moment . . . wait . . . no, that moment . . . and it keeps going on and on, one moment after another, connections linking together. If you leave the event saying, "That was an amazing time, a great event," I venture that you had a fantastic human experience. Someone drew out excitement in you; you tapped into yourself and connected with others. You got off your island, out from under your umbrella, and experienced a great adventure. And you were proud of that stage dive! Those with you caught and supported you. It was improvisation at work.

In his book *The Power of Now*, Eckhart Tolle explores being immersed in the moment. Among other things, he explains that not being able to stop thinking is a dreadful affliction, that connectedness to our mind has become the norm but is also the cause of missing out on our true self. He says that when you connect with your mind, it perpetuates the belief that you are separate from others, that there is a disconnect from your true self. There is a you, and there is everyone else. When we practice the power of *Now*, this overthinking tends to disappear, and we live in the moment and connect with the people around us. By letting go of the mind, we can better connect with our true selves. Our mind is quieted, and we are more likely to have a joyful experience. And we are better prepared to practice and receive sincere hospitality.

I have personally discovered time and time again that thinking gets in my way. If we do as Mr. Tolle advises by toning down our thinking and allowing the hospitalitarian in us to make connections, then we can discover "that all the things that truly matter—beauty, love, creativity, joy, inner peace—arise from beyond the mind."[3] Farmers, astronomers, gardeners, and artists know this. They can quiet their mind and enjoy their work. When you genuinely make a connection, you are silencing your mind. Once you quiet that judging mind, you are more aware, opportunities open up, and you are more receptive to these opportunities. You do not judge, you listen (to yourself and others), even empathize, and most importantly, share in moments both joyful and difficult. You can then become more deeply satisfied. For not thinking much, Mr. Tolle sure is a smart guy.

I once had a staff member named Robin who knew me pretty well. One day she asked me how much time I spent meditating. I was a young manager, and the question took me by surprise. I responded that I had read about meditation, but I hadn't taken the time to practice it. Her response surprised me as well. She basically told me that she thought that I meditated frequently but didn't know I was doing it. I knew that I thought things over quite a bit before I acted and that I had an active mind-life, but I had never considered myself to be in a meditative state. These two principles seem to be opposed. After all, meditation is the quieting of the mind. In later years, I had another friend state that she thought that I was very self-aware. I took that as being self-conscious at the time, but as I look back on it, I think she meant I knew myself and what I stood for, that I had a sense of confidence in who I was. For whatever reason, Robin's and Michelle's comments stayed with me, a perception of me that caught me by surprise.

Oddly, as a practicing hospitalitarian, I don't care for idle chitchat. Filling a room with chatter just to fill the space is an irritation to me. I respect and have a fondness for silence. In the past, I had always chalked this up to what I do for a living. I was talking and listening with staff members and guests for ten to twelve hours a day. Once I was done working for the day, I desired quiet to help recenter myself.

I once knew a couple, and each waited tables at two different restaurants in San Francisco. They once told me they had a rule that neither of them said a word to the other for the first thirty minutes after a shift. They had discovered that this was when they had the most arguments. After getting information overload for hours, it was best to be silent and unwind before they engaged in conversation. They shared a car, so as one picked up the other from the shift, it was a quiet ride home over the Bay Bridge. I think this was a smart move, and I think I needed this too. Was my meditation just being quiet and relaxing my senses on my walk home or on long motorcycle rides? I don't think I know enough about it to say yes, but I am good at spending time thinking about nothing in particular, whenever I get a chance.

I guess, in a way, I was fortunate to be predisposed to taking Mr. Tolle's advice. I can oftentimes let go easily, and I am still working on not judging. In a way, it was how I was brought up, a part of my DNA. At work, I was happy to see anyone who walked through our door—especially if they were on time for their reservation. After a night of being fully present and giving each person my full attention, I would leave work exhausted but also giddy, floating a few inches off the ground in delight as I walked quietly up the steep incline of Bush Street to get to my apartment at Mason Street.

Perhaps there is more to this than just commanding yourself to live in the moment. In order to truly and honestly be in the moment, perhaps you first need to set yourself up for success. You need to come from a place of integrity and honesty with yourself before you can be honest with others. Like using an oxygen mask in an airplane, you must first make sure you are safe so that you can make others safe. Karen McNeil used to call getting oneself in a space to treat others well "setting the tone." While she was writing her book *The Wine Bible*, she was also consulting with restaurants on correct service and hospitality.

Karen suggested that at the end of the pre-shift staff meeting, the staff take thirty seconds to set the tone within themselves in total silence. Each staff member could take the time to focus on whatever they felt they needed to work on: getting out of a grumpy mood, not making any mistakes in ordering, trying to sell more cocktails before the wine (and getting a bigger tip). It could be anything. It was taking time to psych ourselves up for the shift. In my opinion it was also a good transition tool; it got our minds off our outside life and focused on the fun ahead.

The Four Agreements

In his small but mighty book *The Four Agreements*, don Miguel Ruiz describes how he was handed down the lessons that he terms the Four Agreements from ancient Toltec knowledge. I don't want to be a spoiler by diving into his book too deeply, but I would like to share some takeaways that can help you with everyday hospitality—and can help you live a rich life. I also highly recommend that you read the book yourself to get what *you* need from it. I am a firm believer that paying attention to concepts that can make life richer is worthy of your time and attention. After all, you can always discard them later if they don't work out.

The Four Agreements are agreements that you make with yourself. Each is a handshake between you and you. I have found that if followed, the agreements can help free you from some of life's difficulties. Welcoming the agreements is about making new promises and releasing ego-driven agreements that aren't working for you. This is not easily done.

The agreements are:

1. Be impeccable with your word.

2. Don't take anything personally.

3. Don't make assumptions.

4. Always do your best.

Be Impeccable with Your Word

This first agreement is the most important and the foundation for all other agreements. It sounds easy enough but can be difficult. This agreement can also be quite powerful when mastered. It can harm, and it can raise up. As you have discovered when you are in crisis mode, the right words can be important. Your words can create events in people's lives. In hospitality, the same is true.

The word *impeccable* is the key here. Commonly accepted definitions of the word are "faultless" and "in accordance with the highest standards." This sounds tricky. Does being impeccable with our word allow us to say with honesty what's on our mind? Not necessarily, right? Notice the word *faultless* again. Without fault, no judgment, no one is at fault. Being impeccable is also not saying something just to be nice. It's not about trying to be liked or getting back at someone who has wronged you. I believe it's about saying something that has meaning to both you and the person you are saying it to. It's about getting out from underneath your own ego umbrella and not judging yourself or others. It's about connection. It's about doing no harm. When I am impeccable with my word, I want to engage with myself before I speak. Are the words that I am choosing unifying or divisive? Coming from my head or my heart? It's emotional intelligence. It's about gaining the capacity and awareness to control fear and engage others with empathy. Words are powerful. Ruiz talks about how Hitler used words to activate fear. This technique could also easily be used by a politician, boss, or other person in power trying to sway opinion through fear or untruths. You could have someone's best interest at heart, but word choices and how you approach the communication are paramount to how it will be perceived and received. As you practice this agreement, you will make mistakes. When you mess up, you fess up and move on.

Being impeccable with your word works in two directions. You don't say demeaning things about *yourself* or anyone else. You are honest with yourself and others, and you are quick with words of forgiveness because you forgive more easily.

Guests and others often request advice from us, thinking we in the hospitality industry are experts in food, wine, and any "can't miss" sights in the area. In our lives, we often have the power to sway people's choices. In a restaurant, we can direct a guest to an item on the menu that the chef wants to sell or a more expensive item. Or if you are listening and being impeccable, you can guide them to what they may really want. True hospitality is about asking questions and guiding people in the direction that you think best suits them because you have made a connection—no matter how small—with them. If you can guide them to an item on the menu that they would enjoy *and* that the chef would like you to sell, it's a win-win, the cherry on top.

Quite often the best answer to any struggle isn't found until the state of win-win has been reached. "Why live in the *or* when you can live in the *and*," someone once told me. Don't spend time thinking, "Should I do this or that?" or "Should I help make this person happy or this other person happy?" Why decide? Find a way to make everyone happy. Think outside the box.

According to Ruiz, "Every human is a magician, and we can either put a spell on someone with our word, or release someone from a spell. We have the ability to cast spells all the time with our opinion."[4] Yes, your word has power. Every waking moment you have countless opportunities to cast your spells. But you'll have to decide if you'll be a good witch or a bad witch. If you choose, you can cast delightful spells all day long, such as offering to help someone whose arms are loaded with packages. You can surprise someone you are thinking of with a simple text or by taking the time to send a thank-you note.

There are also far bigger ways to use words: sitting, talking, and listening to a friend going through turmoil; reading to the elderly or children; letting someone know that you truly forgive them, when they have attempted to wrong you (I say attempted because no one can wrong you without your consent; you first have to see it as a wrong and agree to it); or throwing embarrassment aside and asking for forgiveness when you have wronged another.

In the hospitality industry, the biggest challenges usually come in the way of anger from a guest or within us. A guest or customer may tear you apart, call you names, or threaten your job. In times like this, the integrity that you have built up over time can be shaken. Don't take it personally (#2 in our list of agreements), and keep in mind that you have several tools to handle the situation. First of all, you are in the hospitality business, not the revenge business, so fighting back is not an option (plus, it says in our restaurant handbook that we never punch a guest). Instead of being snarky, you listen and choose your words calmly and carefully. If the language becomes abusive and I see no other way out, I reserve a line that I have taken from the Ritz-Carlton: "Sir/Madam, we are ladies and gentlemen serving ladies and gentlemen." And I add, "I sincerely want to resolve your problem, and I need you to work with me." To me, this statement has integrity by setting a tone and elevating a deteriorating conversation or diatribe into a civil dialogue. Sincerely wanting to help the guest and being impeccable with your word can break a dark spell that has been cast on someone, even if the spell was cast outside of your realm.

Think about the last time you snapped at someone because they were doing something that was irritating or caused you to be upset. On the occasions that I snap, it is generally not due to anyone's actions. Usually it is due to a mood or something that happened earlier that is still preying on my mind, or I'm tired and cranky. Generally, before I react and start using words, it's a good idea for me to check in with myself and see what is up. In any emotional situation, only after you check in can you answer impeccably. Saying, "Sorry, I am quite distracted by something that happened today. I'm not going to be able to answer your questions in the best way. I need a few minutes" is better than saying, "Stop asking me so many questions, it's annoying!" You need to check in with yourself before you speak, and speak from your heart with integrity whenever possible. It's about accountability.

Many of us have exhausting jobs and work long hours. Managers in restaurants, hotels, and other businesses can quite often not get two days off in a row. This can be draining, and exhaustion can creep in. I once worked fifty-eight days in a row at the Starlight Room in San Francisco (ego). I was no good to anyone. My eyes had bags under the bags, and anger was quick to come. My best friend David O'Malley and I used to remark on how different and light we felt after taking a well-deserved vacation. It was very noticeable, like night and day. Gravity was no longer bowing us to the earth; our heads were up. We were lighter, more optimistic, hopeful.

After one vacation, I told myself that I was going to hold on to that feeling for as long as I could. It lasted a week, two weeks at the most. Then I was back into the same routine, head down and making things happen. Don't get me wrong, there was no black cloud following me around. I just missed the lightness, the optimism that came with being well rested. My energy was low, and I had a shovel in hand, digging deeper into my reserves, which were being quickly depleted.

Don Miguel Ruiz teaches us that "being impeccable with your word is the correct use of your energy: it means to use your energy in the direction of truth and love for yourself."[5] Again, put your own mask on first; if you don't give yourself oxygen, you can't properly oxygenate others.

Being impeccable means not using your word against yourself and helping keep your energy at a higher level. You can call it self-love, respect, or what you will, but be sure to treat yourself well. Treating yourself well and being impeccable with your words can save you valuable energy and keep your batteries fully charged. Our life force— what the Hawaiians call *mana*—benefits from being impeccable. The word is the most powerful tool we have as humans. Consequently, we should use this power only for good.

I can't remember who, but someone wise once taught me about the beach ball theory, which goes like this: Ask several people to sit in a circle. Then place a beach ball in the center of the circle. Ask each person what color the beach ball is. One person might say white and black. Another might say blue and orange. A third might say yellow and green. Who is right? They all have a piece of the story, but none have the full picture. If you rotate the ball a few degrees, you may get a response like, "Hey, now I see what he meant. He was right too." Truth is, you only understand the beach ball fully when you see it from above. The full-color spectrum provides the full perspective.

You must always remember that your opinion is exactly that: *your* opinion or perception. You should not cast it onto others disrespectfully. It's a snowball that you have formed from the information that you have chosen to hold. It's not a representation of all the snow on the earth. It is not the complete truth, even for the person who formed it. It is based on life experiences, perception, a specific reality. It is steeped in perspective. When you take on an opinion, it's a choice. You actively choose to take on that opinion as your own. You can also decide to shed an opinion that does not serve you. In my opinion, your opinion should not be thrown at others like a snowball. You can offer to share it, yes, but you should refrain from throwing it.

Your opinions come from your own point of view, your beliefs, your ego, your dreams for yourself. Your opinion can be poison or quite helpful to yourself or others when put into word form: "That's stupid"; "I can't do that, it's too hard"; "I sure am glad that I got to see you today." These statements all have power. It's nice when people agree with us and our opinion; it makes us feel good. However, we need to be careful with our words. "We create all this poison and spread it to others just so we can feel right about our own point of view," says Ruiz.[6]

Be impeccable with your words. Doing so can be difficult, challenging, and rewarding. Practice every day and see how you feel. If you slip or falter, brush it off and continue. Make mistakes, apologize if necessary, and move on, and you'll get better and better each day, week, and year. Being impeccable with your word with each other is a human experience, and I believe that each of us would prefer a positive human experience.

Don't Take Anything Personally

Ask yourself, does anyone know you better than you? If the answer is yes, then you need to take yourself on a long vacation and examine how you got there. Most people would say no, I know myself best. If no one knows you as well as you know yourself, you have a built-in protection against others' opinions: "You don't know me!" If implemented, this agreement of not taking anything personally could greatly reduce the incidences of getting your feelings hurt and becoming defensive. This is a great agreement for hospitalitarians. We can wear it like a suit of armor under our uniform.

A uniform can be a good suit of armor too. When you are in the uniform of your workplace, you are a representative of the company you work for. When someone speaks to you as a professional, you can choose to take it as "they are not speaking to me personally" or "they are speaking to a representative of my workplace." There's no reason to take anything personally while at work, right?

If no one coming into your business or life knows you as well as you know yourself, no one can put a chink in your armor unless you choose to accept their words as your truth. If you end up taking their words personally, you do so because you choose to. That's right, it's a choice. According to Ruiz, the reason that you choose to take things personally is because of self-importance. It's your ego. He explains that self-importance or personal importance is the maximum display of selfishness because we make the assumption that everything is about us. In truth, nothing anyone else does or says is because of you. Any kind of comment—good or bad—has to do with their perception and not the truth about you or others. Even when directed at you, the comment is still coming from agreements that they have made in their own mind with themselves. You can choose to leave it where it is or take it on yourself.

On the Big Island of Hawaii at Honaunau, this lesson was driven profoundly home for me. Pu'uhonua O Hōnaunau park is a very special and sacred place. It is also a great location to scuba dive from shore. You can see lots of turtles, colorful fish, and moray eels by snorkeling or diving a few yards offshore. I planned to meet friends there for a dive one morning. When I arrived, my friends were standing in the parking lot with a local, whom I recognized from my previous visits. The land is designated open to the public, but the same family had been living on it for many generations. They loved and respected the land as caretakers and had to deal with many "guests" coming to their ancestral land each day. They also tried to pass this respect on to the visitors through dialogue. This information was generally presented in an open, educational manner. It was intended to help share the love and respect for the land whenever visitors were seen doing something that endangered or degraded the area. The caretaker had reminded me on at least one occasion to be careful with my tanks on the lava. His ancestors had spent generations fishing from a section of the lava flow that jetted into the bay. Metal tanks can do damage to lava.

After parking, I walked over to join my friends, who had parked their van in an area closer to the water. I could see that something wasn't right. The body language was not friendly.

As I approached, I could hear the local telling my friends that his family's bones were on these shores, and he asked them to please respect the land by not parking where they had. I felt uncomfortable because I liked and respected the local man, and my friends were being a little overly self-righteous and more than a bit *haoli* (a local term for those that were not native, often white). They were arguing that it was public land and they had every right to park where they had parked.

As the back and forth continued, the local sensed the discomfort in me as I tried to compromise with my friends. He finally turned to me and gave me his full attention. He said something to the effect of, "Bruddah, I can see that you are uncomfortable. Don't take on these people's negative energy. It's them that has to carry it and live with it; let it go."

What freedom I felt! I have tried to live by his suggestion ever since. Talk about the power of words. I didn't need to take on other people's baggage; I could let go and not take the encounter personally. If I were to extrapolate further, I didn't even need to carry my own baggage, for that matter; it was a choice I alone made. If you feed yourself the emotional garbage people toss about, you will become sick. You have the choice not to internalize it and leave it for them to dispose of. You can also dispose of your own emotional garbage.

Kahu Billy was assigned as our spiritual leader at Four Seasons Hualalai. I learned much from him in the time that I was there. Kahu Billy used to marvel at the fact that he was the only paid employee who was not responsible for helping the resort produce some type of revenue; he was the property's spiritual guide. Every week, we would have *mālama* time, a time to care for, serve, or honor, when the staff could talk about anything they wanted with those attending. Kahu Billy acted as a moderator and leader of the discussions. We discussed everything from problems with coworkers to events happening around us.

One sad thing happening was a new resort being built next door, and they were poaching some of our favorite people. We were afraid of losing the people we cared about. Kahu Billy told us a story that happened to him as a way of relieving our sadness and giving us the tools to help us cope.

He told us that when he was driving down the hill that morning, he again noticed the cranes at the new resort disturbing the beautiful view, and he remembered that his wife was mad at him, and he wondered how he was going to pay for the new roof they needed. He then acknowledged that many people loved and supported him at Hualalai. It was a very happy and safe place for him. He loved coming to work and seeing his friends. He decided to put his unhappy thoughts into a bag. On his way down the drive, he threw the bag with the bad thoughts into the lava. That way, he could enjoy his time at work without worries. He had a great day. After work, if he wanted to pick up his worries, he could; he knew where they were. On his way home, he left the bag of worries where it had landed, knowing that if he missed them, he could pick them up the next day.

It is never good to send yourself poison or let others send you poison. Ditch the need to be accepted by those who are not serving your better self. Show your integrity in actions and words, not buying into anything you feel does not serve your individuality well. It's someone else's problem if it is generated by them. Always try to respond with kindness, especially to yourself. If the poison is generated by you, bag it, tag it, and take responsibility for it. You can carry it with you if it serves you or dispose of it when it does not. Forgive yourself; you are human. Celebrate mistakes and learning. Laugh with yourself over misadventures. Live without fear, without fear of the opinions of others. Without fear of failing. Without fear of looking silly. Stop defending yourself. Find the inner spirit and be who you are, or who you choose to be. Fake it till you make it if you need to, but *do it*.

If you live without fear, then you abandon negative emotions. You feel good. When you feel good, things around you seem great, and greatness is attracted to you. You are happy and content with your life. Then when someone wants to dump their poison on you, you say, "That's not mine, that's yours," and you send it away. If something doesn't serve you, get rid of it.

Even if people tell you how wonderful you are, don't take it personally. If you hear it often, don't let it feed your ego. This is also about them and not about you. My very supportive parents always told me how great I was growing up. When they didn't, I felt that I had done something wrong. Then I sought out more compliments. If I had taken their compliments as coming from them, as opposed to about me, I would have wasted a lot less energy seeking approval and just got on having fun.

It is great to be generous with compliments. I always try to simply thank people for their kind words at the time rather than return a compliment. It seems more genuine to me. Then when I notice something about them that pleases me, I can point it out. This way it comes from the heart and is not a tit-for-tat exchange.

"Do unto others as you would have them do unto you," is the golden rule. Oddly, I see this as problematic, simply because, again, you are treating people how *you* want to be treated without regard to how they feel about it. I have adopted a couple of alternate personal "golden rules." One of them is "If everybody did it, would the world be a better place?" The other is "Do no harm." If we look at these first two agreements in the context of *these* golden rules, they come into focus a bit more. If everyone was impeccable with their words and we did not take anything personally, would the world be a better place? Sounds pretty straightforward to me, no harm done.

Don't Make Assumptions

You likely know the saying, When you assume, you make an ass out of U and me. It perhaps is not the lesson you would feel comfortable teaching your eleven-year-old, but it does make a point. Every day we assume, we judge, we take things personally, and the drama begins or continues. And the drama is based on a guess, a deduction, a theory, a hypothesis, a feeling. How many detective novels have you read in which the first assumed bad guy wasn't the one who did it? It's always the one that you least suspect, right? There are life lessons to be learned from pulp fiction.

When we assume, we believe our assumption is the truth, and we can defend those assumptions. We may think, "That guy has a Rolex. He is wealthy." Or "That is an unhappy person. Look at her frown."

Often when I'm deep in thought, people will ask me what's wrong. Usually nothing is wrong; I had just shut off the world for a moment and was not my usual outgoing self. I'm not sad or grumpy; my mind is elsewhere. We tend to see what we want to see. Then we assume that we are right and close the door to seeing what is really true. It's best not to assume, stay open to feedback, and not be so quick to judge. Or as author Neale Donald Walsch puts it in book three of his series, *Conversations with God*, "Increase your observational skills, see what is so, then do what works."[7]

I like Mr. Walsch's/God's words so much that I had them printed on note cards that I carry with me every day in my note pad. Every time I take out my pad to jot a note on one of the cards—which is often because if I don't write something down, I'll most likely forget—I am reminded of this wisdom. If you increase your observational skills, you tend to throw assumptions out the window. You become Sherlock Holmes. You are continually watching—without judgment—and putting clues together. In *The Sign of the Four*, Sherlock asks, "How often have I said to you that when you have eliminated the impossible, whatever remains, however improbable, must be the truth?"[8] As you increase your observational skills, you get closer to the truth, a common or personal truth.

Next, you see what is really *so*. It is then that you can act on what will truly work in that situation. It takes intention, effort, patience with attention to detail . . . and asking questions.

When I go out to dinner, I can sometimes be a less-than-perfect dining companion. I can get distracted watching service and hospitality happening around me because it gives me joy. I will usually choose to sit with my back to the room to help me with my powers of concentration—or lack of. Overall, I believe that I am an amiable dining companion, but there are one or two things that can raise my ire. One is when a restaurant has missed a point of service and their remedy is to offer a complimentary dessert. "Sorry your steak took so long. Dessert is on us." "Sorry we were so late seating you. Dessert is on us." "Sorry for spilling that martini on your head. Dessert is on us." For many restaurants, it's the easy way out, the escape hatch, and it infuriates me because they assume everyone wants dessert.

I feel that it is much more enlightening to empower the staff to read any situation and not assume that there is one fix for everything. If I was having a nice drink at the bar with an appetizer while I waited for my table, I may not mind being seated late. If the steak is a problem, don't charge me for the steak, or simply apologize and replace it. Offering a dessert as a Band-Aid to fix the boo-boo is not truly seeing what is so or doing what works. It's an assumption and more likely falls under the category "doing what's easy."

Also of importance is that offering dessert shows little personalization or effort. It's like getting your spouse flowers every time you mess up. It loses its potency, and it no longer has the intended effect. And by handing out free desserts you are potentially abusing and diminishing the poor pastry cook and his or her amazing creations by giving them away as a fix for mistakes.

On the other hand, we sometimes have a habit of assuming that people know what we want. This happens in all forms of relationships. One person in the relationship is incredulous that another didn't take into account their feelings or know what would ease the problem. Misunderstandings can stem from this. You may hear, "I didn't want you to fix it. I wanted you to listen."

When this happens, were our observation skills waning? Or was it an assumption on their part that everyone should know what they want? Most likely both, right? In this case it is likely that both people were assuming. One had the idea that the other would know what they want, and the second person thought that they were asking for a fix. They were living in Fort Assumption. They were safe with their assumptions, it was comfortable, until it wasn't, because what they thought wasn't true. Luckily there is a key to exit the fort—it's the antidote to assumptions; just ask questions. Once you ask questions, the doors open wide. Sometimes you don't have the courage to ask questions. You may be afraid of the answer or believe that you already know the correct answer or worry asking would make you feel silly. Or maybe you can't be bothered or you're too busy or you believe that if it's not your problem you don't need to worry about it. You make the assumption that everyone thinks as you do (back to the flawed golden rule). You believe they have similar goals, they want to live the way you do, and they feel the way you do. As hospitalitarians—as humans—we need to ask questions to get to how to best help others.

While you are asking questions, you should also be asking for what you need and not assuming that others are not interested. Alternatively, others have already made up their mind about your needs. The worst thing that can happen when you ask for something is that someone will say no. No harm, no foul—at least you asked for what you needed. But if you assume that you don't deserve it, or that another will not be generous, you are only hurting yourself. By not asking for what you want, you are also not allowing others to experience expressing their generosity (hospitality) for you. What a great feeling, helping another human being, and what a great feeling, letting someone help you. In a way, allowing others to give is the cornerstone of the hospitality world. Why would we want to deny another that pleasure? Find your voice, ask for what you want, and when you get a reply, take it as a reply without attachment.

Don't assume or take it personally. Try not to attach value to the answer or your happiness to an outcome. You may feel disappointed by the answer in the short term but not nearly as disappointed as not knowing, not asking. Often, in my experience, these short-term disappointments can turn into hidden jewels over time. As opportunities fade, others appear to take their place. Especially opportunities to help another.

When someone else is asking for something from you, don't assume that they are asking for exactly what they want. Ask deeper questions to find out what they really want. How often have we heard the phrase "Are you busy?" Is that the real question, or is there more behind the question? Often the initial question is a setup for the real question; this happens all the time.

If someone asks for something in a personal setting, you can say yes or no and most people will be OK. If it is in a professional setting, these simple responses are quite often not taken the same way. I have challenged many of the people I have worked with over the years to eliminate the words "no," "don't," and "can't" from their vocabulary. Instead of a negative, use words that offer what you can do for someone. When a guest calls for a reservation, instead of saying, "I don't have that time available," you could say, "I have seven thirty or eight o'clock available for two." If pressed, you could say, "I'm sorry we are fully committed at that time; however, I have an opening the following day at that time."

In a personal relationship, you could say something to the effect of, "I think that I would enjoy a movie more on another night. Is there anything else that you would like to do tonight?" This has more integrity than "I don't feel like a movie" and will probably be better received. This could sound fake or corny until you get used to it. The point is that you should not assume that your guests or people in your life are locked into things they ask for. If you know this, you can respond in a way that extends the conversation instead of building walls and injecting disappointment or resentment. This is a good path to "doing what works." It is also our responsibility to help find a path that works best for everyone involved. Make it a win-win.

To summarize, if you don't understand something, ask questions. If you think you understand, ask questions to help you understand better. This practical practice will help increase your observation skills. Once we stop assuming and communicate positively, we open up many more enjoyable experiences. We communicate cleanly, with integrity, free from emotional poison.

Always Do Your Best

Ruiz's last agreement is about the action of the first three. Do your best at being impeccable with your words, not taking anything personally, and not making assumptions. Always do your best, no more, no less. Please understand that this is a variable. On some days, your best is going to be better than others. But do your best today. Then again tomorrow and each day after. Don't get down on yourself or celebrate too heavily. After all, you were only doing your best.

What is our best? Each day our best is different. Some days are more productive, some days are moody. Instinctively, we know what our best for any given moment can be. If we continue to give our best, day in and day out, we can become less grouchy and more consistent. Take charge; maintain your ability to do your best as it suits each day. When we make a mistake, we do our best to make up for it. We are human, and we are fallible.

Doing your best is also about balance. Your best could be taking time to recharge your batteries. You are responsible for leading a healthy and balanced life. If you are depleted, continue to do your best. Otherwise, you will be disappointed and have regret. Do your best when you are sick, tired, frustrated, or angry. When you do your best, you have no opportunity to become the judge of yourself because you did your best. You know when you have done your best. When you overdo things, when you try to do more than your best, you deplete your body and harm yourself. Just do your best in any circumstances in life and live without regret.

There is an intensity to living your life by doing your best. You become more productive. You can look back and be astonished at what you have accomplished. Writing this book has done that for me. I knew what I wanted as far as an outcome in a general way. But all the little details were very daunting. I had never written a book, but I knew I had a story to tell. I procrastinated (not doing my best) and made excuses and postponed. Finally, things clicked. I did my best every day, and slowly, the cloud lifted. I know I will have to go over these pages again and again. Edit, delete, wordsmith, make sense of nonsense, and explain myself better. But I continue to do my best—most days. I have incorporated fun into these writing sessions. Currently, I'm sitting at Cadet in Napa, my favorite spot for experiencing great hospitality. I'm having a Mare Island Stout to great music. It's cold outside, but I don't mind. I don't want to take up a table inside on a busy Friday night after Thanksgiving. Yes, I'm writing this section on Black Friday night with a delicious black beer. Fun! I'm doing my best!

When you do your best, you are good to yourself. Everyone around you benefits. Your family, your community, your place of work sees you doing your best. This will make you very happy. You do your best because you love it and it feels good. The reward is internal.

When you are doing your best, you are not trying to please your inner judge or other people. In fact, you may disappoint other people when you do your best, but that's OK. If your best isn't good enough for someone, that's not something you need to own. You can always make adjustments and try to get different results—if you choose to. If you do, you try your best in a new way. There should be no judgment about how you were doing it before.

Please know, this is not about lack of accountability. This is about doing your best and keeping the other three agreements with yourself: being impeccable with your word, not taking things personally, and asking questions and not making assumptions. If all the above happen and you are still not able to appease your boss, a significant other, a guest, or a friend, the issue most likely is not about you and never was. Perhaps it's time to reevaluate that relationship.

Taking action and doing your best is about living life fully each day, without fear. Not doing your best is about denying life and bowing to fears. Take a risk, enjoy life. You don't have to prove anything to anyone. Enjoy your life; bring that joy to others.

When I was an instructor at the Culinary Institute of America, we began by teaching service and hospitality in a classroom. Later we entered the restaurant and began performing the concepts and practices that we had learned. We were teaching the future chefs of America how to serve and give great hospitality to our guests. They had signed up to learn how to cook, and many were shy about talking with guests and nervous about handling plates and performing the sequence of service. Others had previous careers as servers or bartenders. We had a wide variety of experiences going out to serve the public each day at Greystone in Napa Valley.

All I asked was for two things to happen: do your best and celebrate your mistakes. We also tried not to make the same mistake twice. My theory was that eventually, we would run out of mistakes. At the end of the shift, we came together and shared the "lame" things that we did. It was almost a contest to see who messed up more. Most mistakes had to do with service points that the guest didn't notice. Once in a while, we really messed up, and one time a guest had to leave without getting their entree. When this happened, there was still a lesson in trying to make up for it. The previous courses and wine were on us. We offered to have them come back and give us a second chance after much apologizing. Some may have tried to blame the kitchen, but they were also in training and doing their best. When we win as a team, we celebrate. When we don't succeed, we all take responsibility.

Years ago, I was given this lesson by a manager at Tra Vigna, a restaurant that was located in St. Helena, in the heart of Napa Valley. As always, the restaurant was busy; we were a group of four and were seated in a booth overlooking much of the restaurant. After being seated, we waited for some time without being acknowledged by anyone.

Finally, a manager came over with a pitcher, apologized, and filled our glasses with cool water on this very warm day. While he was apologizing, I inserted that it was OK; I had noticed that the bussers were busy and that it wasn't their fault. He corrected me. He explained that when the restaurant received accolades, all joined in to receive those accolades because it takes a team to make a great experience. When things go poorly for a guest, they all take responsibility as well. No blaming or finger-pointing, they were on the same team. This struck me. If we all take credit for great recognition, why wouldn't we all take responsibility for any mishaps? If we are observant and doing our best, we will see the holes, and we can make adjustments. Doing so could take a few minutes, but in this case, it was addressed, so why point fingers. The team was treating each other with great hospitality. If this philosophy is the prevalent philosophy of an organization, the workplace becomes a sanctuary where the staff feel safe because they know that they are being supported by the person standing next to them.

If you want to do your best every day, then practice. Repetition is your friend. When it becomes a habit, then you become the master. Whenever I start something daunting and new, it takes me awhile to work through it. I can remember several times forcing myself to get dressed for an early morning run. I would wake up to an alarm, get dressed, tie my shoes, and head out the door, oftentimes without thinking about it. I was afraid if I thought about what I was doing, if I hesitated, I would talk myself out of getting the exercise, especially after closing a restaurant the night before. After several weeks of this zombie-like behavior, I began to look forward to it. Before I knew it, I was near the end of my training, running fifteen-mile days and looking forward to my first marathon. Unfortunately for me, running the Maui Marathon never happened. On the day of the race, I was on a flight back to the mainland, but I wasn't disappointed. I had done the work and was ready. I had done my best and had decided to *not* go in favor of helping a friend.

When you do your best, you take action. Like delivering hospitality, put your mind on what you want to achieve and do your best. Do your best in love, do your best in relationships, do your best when delivering great hospitality every day. See what needs to be done. Help the guest take the picture instead of leaving them to their selfie. Help a neighbor carry the new couch into the house. Return your shopping cart. Open the door for anyone. Smile and say hello to everyone. It takes a strong will to do this every day. There will be obstacles to overcome. Every day will hand you reasons to be frustrated or a reason not to try.

Those who can overcome these obstacles within the arena of hospitality can proudly call themselves hospitalitarians. It's not a badge that will give you great recognition among polite society, but those around you will know. They will see that you stand out, and they will be drawn to you. They will know that they enjoy being around you and can depend on you. They may not know why, but they will know that you have a warmth about you, a fire inside you. You are an optimist, always positive, because you are continually doing your best and are not held back by perceived failures.

I say perceived failures because that's all they are—one perception. In truth, our perceived failures are where we learn the most. We learn who we are and what to do. We learn what we are made of. We often surprise ourselves with our accomplishments. "I never thought I would do that," you might say after you have accomplished something amazing, like giving an important presentation, getting a degree, hosting a particularly important and difficult group, or running that first marathon.

Ruiz tells us that when we do our best, we are also kind to ourselves. We don't beat ourselves up for our missteps. If we do, we are only hurting ourselves, and we are no longer doing our best. Instead, we sit in judgment of ourselves and of not being our best. We cannot do our best when we think of ourselves as failing. We need to relieve ourselves from the inner judge and know that our best is relative. We each have our strengths. Each day is different. As we get better at doing our best, everything shifts, and perhaps we become more consistent. Then as we get better and more consistent, our lows are not as low and the bar becomes higher. It becomes less about the desired destination, and we can enjoy the journey.

One day, your best may be the best ever. The next day, your best may be well below that mark. When you do your best each day, you can look in the mirror with pride. With these practices, you can keep yourself from getting down on yourself and falling into that downward spiral of disappointment. You become the medicine man to yourself and others.

I recently had an experience with disappointment, a lesson that I seem to relearn every so often. I was in a downward spiral emotionally, and it seemed to be centered around what was happening at work. I was frustrated that things were not going as well as I had hoped, and I *chose* to let the situation frustrate me. It seemed to me that my staff did not seem engaged and was just going through the motions, punching the clock and getting through the day without proper care for our guests and our business. Details that should have been taken care of were missed. We were getting sloppy, and our busiest months were approaching. It was as if everything within ten feet of me was going great, but the minute I moved around the corner to see how things were going elsewhere, the activities that were perfect a few minutes earlier seemed to fall apart. At least that was my impression, or how I chose to see it. I began to spiral into anger and high frustration. My staff was letting me down. I began to speak to people in a way that I was later ashamed of. At that point, I was letting them down, all in the name of trying to get them to be actively engaged. There is a saying that "a manager is only as good as the operation is in their absence." In other words, if the staff was misbehaving when I was out of sight, then I wasn't a very good manager. And the more I realized this, the more frustrated I became.

It got so bad and I was so angry that I had to have a talk with myself. I realized I was not doing my best. I was being lazy and letting my emotions carry me, and I was justifying my actions to myself. The next day I announced at that morning meeting that I was retiring Eddie Cranky Pants. He was no longer invited to display himself at work. I was turning over a new leaf. I apologized to the staff, and I told them that I enjoyed working with them and I was going to be more joyful. I told myself that I needed to recommit to doing my best.

I found a path that made me and the staff happier. Things began to fall into place. I think the most glaring realization happened a few weeks after my attitude change. I was watching everything flow fairly seamlessly. Overall, the guests were being well cared for, but I saw a few errors happening here and there. Instead of reacting to the unforced errors, it occurred to me that this was the same staff that I was around when I was spiraling out of control with a big black cloud over my head. They were making a few mistakes, but they were doing a great job overall. I had changed my perception (assumptions), and I had changed the way I spoke to them. I was no longer getting angry because I was not taking things so personally. I was happier, and when I was doing my best, the staff enjoyed working with me more—I hope.

A falcon flies better and faster than a song sparrow. It is the best flier in the bird kingdom. But it does not sound nearly as melodic as a song sparrow. We each have our strengths.

CHAPTER 3

The Spirit behind Hospitality

I drink to the days that are.

—WILLIAM MORRIS

I HAVE OFTEN LEFT AN overly long shift exhausted but feeling happy, with sore feet and a spring in my step. Even though gravity has taken its toll, I have a feeling of lightness. My body would weigh me down as I walked home uphill from Bistro Roti on the Embarcadero in San Francisco in my early management days. It was a long march, but for some reason, I usually felt great. It wasn't always like this; some shifts were miserable, and sometimes the hill seemed daunting. Oddly, I seem to have almost forgotten those shifts over time.

I was reminded of this feeling more recently after working a shift at Bottega in Yountville, California. At the time, I was an instructor at the Culinary Institute of America (CIA) by day and helping cover some management shifts on the weekend for Bottega at night. I'd leave the house at seven thirty in the morning for my eight thirty class and teach at the CIA until three thirty. I would then drive to Bottega in time to make the four thirty pre-shift meeting and stay through service. I did this two or three times a week for a few months.

I was exhausted but happy. I attribute this emotion to several factors. Most importantly, I was doing what I love. Unlike my day job, I wasn't teaching; I was doing. Don't get me wrong, I also got a high from teaching, but it was not as intense. Often when I've had this high, I've had great connections with happy guests and staff members. I remember one night walking to my car at eleven thirty p.m. after another long day, feeling quite happy. The guests, the staff, and I had *fun* together that evening. It was fun, but does fun explain why I felt as good as I did? Exercise can get me to this "heady" feeling sometimes, but it doesn't go as deep as what I was feeling. Exercise seems to reside in the physical. This was a more soulful feeling, more than I could get from a good runner's high. My feet hurt, I had bags under my eyes, my brain was tired, I could barely hold a thought, but I felt on top of the world.

I have always been more of a spiritual guy than a religious guy. I was born into a Catholic family and went to church with my parents religiously, but rarely did I go on my own after leaving home. Over my lifetime, I have spent countless hours reading about Buddha, Toltecs, Tao, and Shamanism and have had great conversations with several people about Judaism. I have a deep interest in why, and this journey has helped me formulate my version of why. I was in search of the common thread that runs through these spiritual practices. I love the work that I do, so naturally I began folding some of these concepts found in my readings into my everyday life.

My contemplations eventually led me toward the author Eckhart Tolle. After reading *The Power of Now*, I began to understand my deeper feeling of happiness around these occasions at work. I came to understand that perhaps this blissful feeling was because I was "forced" to stay in the moment, the now, for long periods of time. Because of the intensity of the restaurants I was working in, there would be several hours during a shift when there was no future, no past—only now. For a few amazing hours, I was forced to forget about my burdens, the things I had to do, my relationships, bills, (perceived) mistakes I had made, everything but one thing: what was happening in the moment right in front of me.

During one shift, a woman was upset because we were not living up to her expectations. I met her away from the table on the way to the ladies' room. She was distraught enough to have tears on her face. She explained that she and her husband had planned this trip to Napa for two years and that Chef Chiarello was her favorite chef. This night was supposed to be the highlight of their big anniversary trip, but the waiter didn't care. I listened and told her not to worry, that it was going to be an exceptional experience for her. I suggested that she trust me.

I found out where they were seated and went to her table before she returned. I spoke briefly with her husband and, after learning where they were at in the meal, I formulated a plan. I communicated my plan to the server and ordered an additional appetizer to give myself an excuse to come back to the table and speak further with them about their plans around their trip to Napa. At the time we had shaved raw Brussels sprouts on the menu. It was often ignored because . . . well . . . you get it. But it was delicious. When I walked this unique salad to the table, I explained that they had to try it, even though they may not like Brussels sprouts and may have never tried them raw. Thankfully, they loved it and had an additional great story to tell around their visit. We lavished them with attention and conversations around their plans while in the valley. To top it off, we had some books that had already been signed by the chef in the restaurant, so with dessert, I gave her a signed copy of our book. She then shed tears of happiness, and I felt happy for them. The husband thanked me for the save on the way out of the restaurant with a hundred-dollar bill discreetly placed in my suit pocket, which of course, I split among the server and support staff.

According to Tolle, feelings of joy, love, and moments of deep peace are only possible with gaps in thought. "For most people, such gaps happen rarely and only accidentally, in moments when the mind is rendered 'speechless,' sometimes triggered by great beauty, extreme physical exertion, or even great danger. Suddenly there is an inner stillness, there is a subtle and intense joy, there is love, there is peace." He goes on to say that this feeling cannot flourish until "you have freed yourself from mind dominance."[1]

He continues: "The mind always seeks to deny the Now and escape from it. In other words, the more you identify with your mind, the more you suffer . . . the more you are able to honor and accept the Now, the more you are free of pain, of suffering."[2]

The scenario with the woman and her perceived slight could have gone several ways. I could have taken the stance that we weren't obligated to jump just because she spent the past two years fantasizing about how great we were going to be. Or I could have said, "The server did nothing wrong. You will be taken care of just like everyone else." The thing is they weren't everyone else; no one is everyone else. Each of us is an individual with a different history and life experiences. If I would have taken an alternate path, I believe that it would have been my ego talking, my brain taking over, or just being lazy, which is still ego. (I can't be bothered.) Instead, I empathized with them and stayed in the moment with no past, no future, just now. How can I help now? What can I say now? How can I insert myself now?

Believe me, I'm no saint. I'm not perfect when it comes to making these decisions; that is how I know the difference between good decisions and faulty ones. I have taken the dark road with guests and staff. I have come in hot without knowing the full story and made it worse. And I have seen the outcome, which is usually not good and often embarrassing. It is in our mind's best interest to try to control us. This is where the ego lives. This is where the past and future live. This is where we cling to experiences that we have had, what we may label as good and bad experiences. On occasion, we will go against our minds and do something because we feel we should. Some say that this is our larger purpose calling us. We all have examples of this in our lives. I used to say that I had a bluebird sitting on my shoulder that told me what to do. I later believed it to be intuition. I now think that it may be a connection to the now, which brings forth our inspiration. I can't imagine an artist or athlete who is in the zone thinking about anything else other than the now. I feel that working with hospitality has been my training, perhaps my form of meditation. It has been my larger purpose that helps me to be happier, calmer, more joyful, and centered.

It is not the same for everyone. I worked side by side with coworkers who had other reasons for their choice of vocation—family income, school, flexibility for travel, "income until I get a real job," and the perennial cliché "waiting to be discovered." Restaurants, resorts, and hotels can be a lily pad, a joyful respite for some until they find their higher calling. Often, hospitalitarians will venture out into the real world only to find that they need to return to the tribe. The good news is that we are a clan that will always welcome you back.

If we feel ourselves getting angry or frustrated, oftentimes something out of our past is triggering the memory of the current experience. When this happens, we are not experiencing the now; we are reliving an experience, which has nothing to do with the now. When thoughts arise in your mind like, "I hate it when people are like this," it is your past experiences and judgments dictating the future or, more precisely, the present. The key is to bring yourself back into the moment. Realize that this is your thought and not the reality of the moment. The people in front of you are not anyone but themselves, being themselves.

The great news is that in the vocation of hospitality, you will most likely only be required to deal with any shenanigans from a visiting group for an hour or two, three at most. If you work or live with them, it could be a bit longer, however. The thing to remember is that their behavior is not personal against you. Why not try to do your best and make their experience great? If I try to get out of my mind and back into the moment, quite often the stress and bad feelings dissipate. Maybe at some point with enough practice, this can be our natural state.

Karen McNeil shared a story with a group of us years ago about an experience she had in the DC area. She told us that there was a restaurant that had a team goal of not allowing anyone who arrived stressed or angry to leave that way. If the assigned server could not personally turn someone around, they would ask for the rest of the team to help. While performing their duties, each team member would walk by the table and simply make eye contact and smile. She said that few could resist lightening up with that many happy people giving them recognition.

When we find ourselves in any unpleasant situation, we can be assured that we feel that way because our mind is judging the moment as being unpleasant and attaching that label to the experience. We then choose to accept the agreement with our mind, and our body reacts. When we feel this trigger happening, it is an indication that it is time to get out of the mind and get into the present moment. This has been a great tool for me (when I actually use it), and surprisingly, often the bad scenario (rude guest, flat tire, bad shift, long line) turns out to have benefits—if I am paying attention.

I am quite fond of the saying, "Pay attention to the signposts in life." Pay attention to who and what is around you, and apply your keen observational skills and situational awareness. When I think back, memorable moments in my life happened when I *stopped* listening to my brain. I *did* what I felt I needed to do, what needed to be done. I have also found that added perspective through enhanced observation often means more enjoyment. I have initiated some of the best conversations this way, which have led to many rewarding adventures. When I look back, these experiences are also the most vivid, like a bookmark. I suspect I was clearly in the moment at the time.

Aborigines, Native Americans, and other tribes and cultures believe that the universe will provide for them if they are paying attention. When we are in a state of awareness and food presents itself, it is no coincidence according to this belief. It is the universe providing. Since the animal or plant has given itself to us, it is appropriate for the person receiving the gift to give thanks and respectfully enjoy the gift. Many Indigenous cultures have this courtesy and respect for Mother Earth and her children and search for the signs. If we choose to look deeper, we may begin to see that when we ask, we often receive. Sometimes, the result can be immediately obvious; other times it takes awhile to unfold. Just maybe there is truly no such thing as coincidence in the universe. This can hold true for hospitality as well. Hospitality is about awareness, seeing open doors and walking through them. It's a big-picture concept with attention to the details.

Paying attention to the signposts also applies when circumstances don't go as planned or when all appears against you. When I'm in these situations and if I am paying attention, I can often take a problem and turn it into an opportunity. The Aikido way of changing your opponent's energy to work for you would be a great example: not taking an attack head-on but altering the energy so that it can benefit you.

If you get laid off or fired, keep in mind that there will be better opportunities ahead as other doors open! Perhaps the job wasn't a good fit anyway. Flat tire? Check out that pair of red-tailed hawks flying overhead and feel that cool breeze. Consider the moment a nice break from driving, *and* a flat tire is an excellent reason for being late. For me this approach is not about silver linings or always looking on the bright side of life, even though that is likely what it looks like from the outside. It is more about exploring what is *truly* going on inside me. If you believe that the universe provides, then ask what it is providing for you now. Why did my tire malfunction *now*? What do I need to see or learn or observe at this moment? Why am I frustrated with my situation? Maybe, just slooooowing dooown is the message.

In the example earlier with the couple celebrating their anniversary, the now is what won the evening over for them. Were they living in the now when they were upset? Nope. It was ego and expectations or imagination of what the meal was going to be like. They had set expectations in their mind, in the past, and wanted to play out that scenario in the now. When their experience wasn't what they imagined, they were upset. Who really cares what the waiter thought anyway, right? You can still have a great vacation without the staff joining in. By doing what we did, we brought them back into the now. It was our gift, our way of shifting their perception. We provided good hospitality with intent.

What is so great about now? It is truly all we have. There has never been a time other than now. My memories are my version of a past now, and the future hasn't even happened yet. So if the now is all we have, that is where our focus should be. Using the tools that we have discovered thus far, we can quiet our mind and not live a distracted life void of the now. We can do our best each day to live in each moment and experience everything we can in it, and many of our worries will fall away.

Is this what I was feeling at the great moments in my life? When I am busy at and engaged in hospitality, I know that I feel *alive*. You could say that I am addicted to this feeling. For me there is nothing like it other than maybe riding my motorcycle (fast). I am in my body, in each moment, and time is flexible. It stretches and flies by and then slows down, and a minute behaves like a thirty-minute experience. It's a blast! When I am immersed in delivering great hospitality, I feel no suffering, emotional or otherwise. I have received deep cuts, bumps, and bruises, and I am able to shrug them off as nothing but a scratch. Work is my haven when going through a tough breakup or suffering a loss. Making people happy and living in the moment makes me happy. After all, I will heal; there is time for that.

When I first read Tolle's words that "suffering needs time," I was taken aback. When I am in the now, time gets fuzzy; I have no idea what time it is. Yes, I can get lost in my work. The fun for me has been to have these same experiences in my life. In fact, often, my life and my work are not separated. They often easily flow together. Some can understand this, and others see their work as separate from their lives. I feel that many of us who ply our trade in hospitality get it. Pure hospitality is all about the now: hospitality to yourself, hospitality to others, hospitality in your life.

Eckhart Tolle views all suffering being wrapped around ignoring the now and letting your mind take control. He places the non-now into two categories: clock time and psychological time. When you set goals for yourself or remember a moment in the past, it is called clock time. Clock time can also be used to learn lessons and is how we can remain safe in the now, such as acknowledging that fire can burn you and that you should make sure a ladder is steady before climbing it.

Psychological time is where we get guilt and anxiety and tend to dwell and obsess on things. Also, criticism—both self-criticism and criticism of others—can link us to a false sense of identity in psychological time. If we are in the now, there is no judging. You can still have a goal and honor the moment in each step to achieving that goal.

However, if you obsess about the goal in your mind because you see it as securing your happiness, the now is no longer honored.

In any emergency, the mind tends to stop, and you enter the now. Either you survive or you don't; it's fight or flight. Time seems to slow down; there is only the moment, like single frames in a movie. Or it can speed up and fly by when you are completely immersed in anything that you love to do. Time becomes adjustable, flexible, and everything is temporary. Time has important attributes when practicing hospitality or any craft that you love. We know that the now is ever moving; time as a snapshot is temporary. The day will end. The sun will go down and rise again, so why not have fun and get the most out of now?

The now goes on forever, and it is fleeting. There is a Zen story that I remember about some monks who were imprisoned by a ruler. As I remember, that ruler said that he would release the monks if they would give him something that would cheer him up when he was sad and make him appreciate his happy moments. The monks gave him a ring. The ruler was confused by the ring. He asked the monks to explain. They said, "Read the inscription." On the inside was etched "This too shall pass." All we have is now.

One of Eckhart Tolle's teachings also lines up with something else I believe. When a problem arises, you have two choices. Deal with it now or accept it as something that "Is." To dwell on it or fear it is a waste of time; it can affect us and our ability to be happy. Life is about being happy, being light on your feet and optimistic in knowing that you can resolve any problem or put some icing on someone's cake. When I get overwhelmed or out of my zone (not living in the now), I become easily irritated, and Eddie Cranky Pants wants to come out. People around me, especially those I work or live with, notice this shift in me, and they don't like it. I feel it too—I'm not happy; gravity seems stronger than usual. The worst part is, I *know* it is happening, and sometimes I can't seem to climb out of it. If I don't address it now, eventually "this too shall pass," and I will wake up one day and it will be gone. But why would anyone want to put themselves and others through the waiting? The trick is identifying when it is happening *and* doing something about it now, either accepting it without judgment or addressing it. If we are engaged in any situation in any given moment, then we can decide more easily if we would like to deal with it or accept it. If irritation arises, we are not in the now. When we are focused, we can more easily release our ties to any outcome. Once this happens you are more open to alternate paths. There are no successes or failures; there is learning and living. Clinginess falls away because it has no grip on you. When you feel you are succeeding, you want to cling to this success. When the success wanes and you are disappointed, you are not in the now. Failure and success are the same and should not be tied to your identity. We stay light on our feet and shed negativity. Like Eeyore, the more we project the negative, the more it surrounds us. Negativity can behave like a trigger. When we feel the negativity creeping in, we refocus and bring ourselves back to the present. We can then accept any situation or label it as only temporary; this too shall pass.

In chapter 8 of *Practicing the Power of Now*, Eckhart Tolle finetunes the concept of "this too shall pass" a bit more. He explains that everything comes in cycles and that it is up to us to decide how we deal with the situation. One cycle cannot exist without the other. If we are engaged in the moment, then we have the ability to surrender to what is. When you surrender to what is and you are in the now, the past loses its power. Therefore any irritation goes away. Nothing is permanent. If we cling and resist, we will suffer.

Failure lies concealed in every success, and success is concealed in every failure. Everyone succeeds and fails. We mustn't cling to one or the other. We should manifest and create but not become attached to the outcome. Our successes and failures are not who we are. They are merely our life situation right NOW.

When good things happen, your mind will cling to them and resist any changes. This resistance will make you unhappy. You don't want to lose the good things, and your mind will resist the change. This makes you unhappy in a happy moment. This means that your happiness and unhappiness are indeed one. Happiness and unhappiness are the same. The only difference is time.

To stay in the now is to stay light on our feet, with grace and ease; it's the graceful dance of life. We are free from the stickiness of attachment. We simply don't become attached, we live in the moment and realize that this just *is*. When you are no longer dependent on whether things are going good or bad, they just are. We then lose judgment about our situation. Cycles come and go, life now flows with more ease. Simply *being* can give you nonresistance and a feeling of peace. You may not be happy in the traditional meaning, but you will be at peace and in a better state to be open to the good things coming your way.

Tolle goes on to say that all negativity is a result of resistance. The ego believes that through negativity it can manipulate reality and get what it wants. Your mind believes that through negativity, it can attract a desirable condition. In truth, negativity does not attract a desirable condition; instead, it drives a desirable condition away. Think Eeyore. Negativity keeps an undesirable condition in place, which is why Eeyore's condition never changes. Negativity strengthens the ego, and that is why the ego loves it. "Look what has happened to me, and let me tell you what I am going to do about it," your ego says. Your ego can then identify with your anger and sorrow, and you become this sorrow or anger and sabotage the positive in your life.

If instead you make the choice to focus on becoming more present, you will not need negativity anymore; it can be vanquished. You can toss it to the side. When the negativity appears, use it as a signal—a signal that you need to be more in the present. Negativity can be your voice telling you to *wake up*, pay attention, get out of your mind. When you are irritated, observe it and drop it; it serves no purpose. If you can't drop it, accept it and realize that it has no hold on you, no purpose. Work on this, and you may be able to loosen the hold. With practice, this negativity will begin to pass right through you without being caught in your net. Practice with little things. Realize that your frustration or anger is far more disturbing to you than the irritation that caused it. It's the ego trying to hijack who you really are.

This can become a daily practice. Feel the irritation, come into the present, and watch it disappear. Waiting in long lines can become opportunities to observe and connect, and bad drivers cannot affect your day (unless they slam into you). Your children may need to quiet down to maintain a balanced household, but doesn't the sound of them warm your heart? Especially when you know that this too shall pass; they are young for such a short time. In the miracle of surrender, once you accept it, every moment is the best moment. That sounds like enlightenment to me.

This practice is similar to what an oyster does. The oyster theory tells us that when an oyster feels an irritation such as a grain of sand, it begins a process of wrapping the sand in silica to help smooth it over. As it does so, it turns an irritation into an object of beauty—a pearl. Turning irritation into an experience of beauty seems like a great superpower to me.

Tools can help. For hospitalitarians, most restaurants and hotels give the employees flexibility when it comes to solving irritations. Most of us have the tools to take care of any situation, so why fear? We will do the best we can, right? If you don't have the tools you want, then use the tools you have, or go get new tools.

In the grand scheme, we are quite fortunate today. Many of us have technology, friends, teachers, and community to support and help us. I've had a few life-threatening moments in my life. Each was tolerable because I didn't know that they were life threatening at the time. For me, most negative and transitional experiences have been tolerable. Did they change aspects of my life? Yes. Is this because I had a charmed life? Or is it because of a unique attitude?

Tough money situations have outcomes that are tolerable. Family deaths—I have great memories, I miss them, and they are with me in spirit. Relationships are always kinetic, and any outcome needs to be respected. Health problems and injuries have outcomes too. We can deal with anything in the now or accept the circumstances as our current and temporary position.

I recently found myself in one of these situations. I was without work and laid up for six weeks after a series of surgeries and several days in the hospital. I needed a job but could not work. I had little savings, and my bimonthly unemployment check wasn't going to cover my mortgage. I assessed my situation and realized a few truths. I had spent the last few months getting a new restaurant up and successfully running. It was not my first. In any restaurant opening, you can count on many long days, with few—if any—days off. I loved the adrenaline rush and the feeling of accomplishment in these restaurant openings. But I had not taken care of myself. Long hours, few days off, poor diet, stress, lack of proper exercise, and age had forced my body to put a stop to all this nonsense.

My youthful, fortified bulletproof vest had been retired, and I needed to pay attention to my body. After my hospital stay, I had a few weeks of recovery ahead. I began to realize that I had not had this much time off in a long while. In one way I was truly looking forward to some downtime, and it was too bad I felt so crappy. But I didn't want to waste this opportunity. I began thinking about how I could put the gift of time to use by changing my life for the better. I decided that I didn't need to open restaurants anymore. In my heart, I wanted to put that part of my life into my past. I didn't need to prove anything to myself or anyone else any longer. I simply needed to be happy. Happiness to me was working sane hours, spending time with my daughters, and helping someone grow their business through great hospitality. After more than forty years in the restaurant business, it was time for a change.

I purged some material goods on Craigslist that I had collected over time to help raise money to pay the mortgage. I was also fortunate enough to be able to borrow some money from my brother Tim. Eventually, I was able to picture my ideal job. When thinking about my fictional new job, the factor that resonated most within me was the desire to find a workplace where I could focus on hospitality. I am pretty good with spreadsheets and finances, and I enjoy setting up budgets (and hitting them), but I wanted to immerse myself in these ideas around hospitality. You can call it manifestation or luck—call it what you will—but again, I listened to that little bluebird on my shoulder, and I landed the job that fulfilled this dream.

It happened organically, in a way that not only seemed natural, but for me, deep down, I never entertained a doubt that it would happen. Of course, I had moments of anxiety; the black cloud would begin to form as the panic of what my future looked like crept in. Money was running low. The uncertainty was scary, but at my core—in my heart—I knew I would find my way. The direction felt right. I realized that I wanted to leave the restaurant business and join a winery.

Wineries were not generally open late at night, and it seemed like the perfect platform to ply my hospitality trade. After all, I lived in the Napa Valley. New visitors came to our valley every day, travelers from all over the world. For these guests, coming to wine country was not merely a transaction. They were not there because they needed to eat or make a purchase. They were coming for an experience, pursuing their passion and expanding their knowledge. They wanted to learn about wines, relax, and soak up the beauty. The stage was set.

As I lay on my couch each day recuperating and weaning myself off medication, I filtered through the long list of wineries listed on the Napa Valley Vintners Association website. It took days, which had the added benefit of keeping my mind working and my heart engaged. I would go to each winery's website and see if I was attracted to them. For the few that I connected with, I sent off my resume and a letter stating my intentions. When I got to the Cs, I came across Caymus Vineyards.

I had met Chuck Wagner, the owner and winemaker, in my early management days at Bistro Roti in San Francisco in 1989. He had come in for dinner on occasion, and during one of our conversations, I happened to mention that I had always wanted to learn how to make wine. Chuck being Chuck, he invited me to come visit. He said he would put me to work. I began working with his crew on my off days. I would watch the sunrise as I performed pump-overs in tanks of fermenting wine. He even set me up the following year to come up to Rutherford and pick some grapes. He also set me up with a barrel so that I could try my hand at making some port from some of the grapes we had picked. I enjoyed talking with him and his parents, Charlie and Lorna. They were farmers, and I could relate, having grown up in the great state of Iowa. I think I surprised Chuck when he found out that this San Francisco city boy could drive a tractor.

Decades had passed since those days, and I was hoping that he might remember me. I shot off an email to the general mailbox at Caymus, with a note about my history with Caymus and the Wagners. I told them I was seeking a hospitality position. As it happened, Chuck told one of his executives, Karen Perry, that he wanted to hire a restaurant person to help adjust the way the guest experienced the tastings at Caymus. On the same day, she received my email. Kismet! The interview took about thirty minutes, and I got an offer letter a few days later. I now have the freedom to do what I love, and I am being paid to do it! I go to work each day and pinch myself for my good fortune. Did I work for it? Yes, if you call doing what you love work. But mostly I just listened to my inner self and acted on what it told me. The cool part is that what got me pointed in the right direction was my body telling me in strong terms that I needed a change. When I truly listened, I could see a new path. When I stopped being a human doing and became a human being, I was again living in the now. When I am living in the now, my sense of self is joyful and I am just being who I am. I know this deep within my heart, and it thrills me to be able to recognize this and give credit where credit is due. I love the feeling.

When I am in the moment and not in my head, I am a better listener. I find that my head messes me up and can get me into trouble or into an emotional spiral. But my heart knows what I need. In his book *The Pleasure Prescription*, Paul Pearsall, PhD, tells us that the brain is not the only organ that has the ability to think. Scientists have found that the heart is much more than a pump. They have found evidence that when we say, "In my heart I feel . . . ," we really mean it and are experiencing it. They have found that the heart thinks, feels, and functions much the way that the brain does. The heart, as it turns out, is rich in biological oscillators that help keep the body functioning. The heart is actually a master oscillator that produces electromagnetic signals forty to sixty times greater than the brain. A hormone is secreted from the atrium of the heart that influences our emotional state. This sends off physical and emotional responses even before the brain "knows" that we are having feelings, before it can put together a full thought around what is happening.[3] In other words, our heart can react before our brain even knows that anything is going on. We may never personally know or understand this relationship of the heart fully, but we can begin to shut down our brain a little and listen to our hearts more. Our heart often knows first. For me, listening to my heart takes effort and intent.

How important is it to follow your heart when it comes to making vocational choices? In his book *Tribes*, Seth Godin writes,

> "It turns out that people that like their jobs the most are also the ones who are doing the best work, making the greatest impact and changing the most. Changing the way they see the world . . . also changing the world, by challenging the status quo, a cadre of heretics, discovering that one person, just one, can make a huge difference . . . engaged in work that matters. Heretics are the new leaders, the ones that challenge the status quo, who get out in front . . . who create movements. The marketplace now rewards and embraces the heretics. It's clearly more fun to make the rules . . . and for the first time it is also profitable, powerful, and productive."[4]

Hospitality is about our awareness and connection—awareness of our surroundings, connection to how we are feeling, and having the awareness of what is behind our actions. It is important to identify and be cognizant of whether these actions are creating a stronger connection or simply manipulating the situation. Is there a way for it to be both? I think so. Sometimes we inject hospitality to get people out of their usual choices, out of their comfort zone, for a more memorable experience. Sometimes it is taking that risk, the extra effort that you feel the situation needs. Not just taking the safe path, but purposefully diverting the path for the best effect. Could this be called heretical hospitality? Hmm.

CHAPTER 4

The Culture of Hospitality

"'Heahea! Kāhea 'ai." Welcome!
Come in. Come in and eat.¹

—HAWAIIAN PROVERB

THE UNITED STATES IS blessed with a myriad of cultures
from all over the world. Some cultures are also homegrown.
We hear about—and if lucky—have had the chance to experience Southern hospitality, or the kindness of people from the Midwest,
or from our neighbors in Canada and Mexico. Japan, China, and many
Asian countries are known for their great hospitality, as are other
pockets around the world. There are hospitality belief systems for all
religions of the world as well as cultural hospitality within Indigenous
tribes. People worldwide carry these beliefs and customs with them
when they travel to other lands. When people migrate from their country of origin and settle in a new place, communities develop around
these beliefs. I would hazard a guess that the overarching concept of
hospitality is universal.

The pineapple has been the symbol of hospitality for centuries in the Western world. It found its path to this role through its rarity when sailing ships ruled the seas. For hosts in Europe, the pineapple became an indication of the wealth and status of its possessor and the lengths they would go to impress their guests. Christopher Columbus and his crew were reported to be the first Europeans to have encountered the pineapple in their travels. It looked like a pinecone but ate like an apple with its soft inner fruit. Getting the fruit back to Europe without spoiling was difficult, however. Pineapples did not travel well, as they tended to rot during the hot and rough voyage. The good news was that they were rich in vitamin C, so by consuming them, the crew could stay healthy on the long trip home.

Many in Europe did not know the taste of the fresh pineapple in the decades following its "discovery." Only the fastest ships made it back with fresh pineapple. Dried and candied pineapples were more common in Europe and eventually in the early American colonies. Fresh pineapple was rare and expensive, and some purveyors even rented them to party hosts as an ornament, as most could not afford to purchase them for consumption. You could be reassured that your host or hostess spared no expense when you saw a fresh pineapple as a centerpiece.

Because only a certain class of people could afford a fresh pineapple, craftsmen and artists began making carvings, paintings, castings, and other decorative items that represented pineapples. Door knockers, signs, and even bedpost ornaments were common in inns during the early colonization of America by our European ancestors. The symbol of the pineapple had been transformed from a symbol of status to a symbol of welcoming.

The pineapple currently resides on the throne as the symbol of hospitality. But does this mean that the pineapple has earned the right and is today worthy to represent what hospitality truly means at its core? Doesn't its origins in wealth and prestige differ from the spirit that we are exploring? Isn't the simple ability to afford an item different from the act and intent of sharing yourself with others? Does our exploration of hospitality align with what the pineapple represents, or are we simply carrying the flag of its historical representation? Does it even matter?

I contemplated these questions. I understood and had accepted that the pineapple *was* the symbol for hospitality—my passion. As I contemplated, I eventually came to my own pineapple story. I have a vivid fantasy life.

It may be true that the pineapple began its legendary position as a status symbol of wealth and social standing with our European ancestors, and for those who could not afford to enjoy the flesh of fresh pineapple, the legend became about the iconic shape. The pineapple as a symbol became about the surface, the shape, the "pine" part of the fruit. Before Western man found it, the fruit had a more earthbound existence. It was a sustainer of life. Pineapples provided sustenance, hydration, and vitamin C for those who grew and carried them. It traveled well for some distances due to its rugged exterior. In the beginning, however, its beauty was inside. It was not about the "pine," it was about the "apple"; it was what was inside that counted.

I understand that pineapples hail from South America and grow in many places in the world, but to me and many others, they come from one place in particular: Hawaii. The sun and soil of Hawaii are responsible for forming the inner beauty of the pineapple. If you have ever had fresh-picked pineapple in Hawaii, you will never forget it. It tastes like sun and cool breezes. If the pineapple is the physical representation of hospitality and its most recognized place is the Hawaiian islands, then it stands to reason that the pineapple is acquainted with the energy of the islands, the island culture, and specifically the word "aloha."

In Lawrence H. Fuchs's book *Hawaiian Pono*, he writes, "The Hawaiians spoke of generosity as, 'Hawaiian aloha,' Something that could not be commercialized. Aloha was given freely, not to make money or influence [people]. One Hawaiian admired by his fellow Polynesians on the island of Kauai spoke repeatedly of 'Hawaiian Heart.'" For the Hawaiian people first coming into contact with Asians and Europeans, along with this "Heart" was a lack of understanding of why anyone would lie. "As a leader of Oahu put it, 'The Hawaiians were not double-faced.' Another spokesperson asserted, 'The Hawaiians have no idea what a white lie is.'"[2] It seems that the people of Hawaii had much to teach the world, exhibiting aloha as a standard of conduct. The true spirit of aloha is one of the cornerstones to hospitality.

Aloha means so much to so many people; it has a multitude of connotations depending on the context. It can be a greeting (*hello*) or a parting salutation (*goodbye*). It comes from the heart and is not a specific action, although aloha can be displayed by action. If I were to come up with a definition that speaks to me, I would say aloha is "a unique connection based on love." The connection of one heart to another, one person to another, and as we will learn, one breath to another.

In her all-encompassing (and amazing) book *Managing with Aloha*, Rosa Say put it this way: "Aloha defines the epitome of sincere, gracious, and intuitively perfect customer service [insert "hospitality"] given from one person to another."[3] She believes that the spirit of aloha is the core of Hawaiian belief and that managers of people need to be proactive in embracing its concept or risk thriving.[4] Aloha is that important.

Businesses and relationships thrive when they are healthy. It doesn't matter if you call it aloha or not, a healthy work or life environment will have certain key elements. "Think of aloha as an attitude—a good attitude. Aloha is an attitude that is positive, inclusive, and healthy, for the pure love of it. Aloha permeates your company because all of your employees and all of your peers feel the same way: they treat each other with honesty, openness, trust, dignity, and respect. They freely share the caring and love of Aloha with each other, and so naturally, they treat [their guests] that way too."[5] I love the idea of creating a culture that unconditionally takes care of each other so that taking care of those around them is merely a continuation of the flow.

Aloha can radiate unmentioned during any conversation, and you can receive it every day. It can be projected, like a breath. You can witness it in someone's eyes or a genuine smile. Everything we have spoken of to this point is wrapped around aloha—living in the now, not becoming irritated by small things, and being connected to those around you. It's a total lack of judgment, not taking things personally, being impeccable with your word, doing the best you can, and not making assumptions. This is why this word is so powerful. It is pure love: love for yourself and others.

Rosa Say further defines aloha as "the value of unconditional love. The outpouring and receiving of the spirit. It's an expression of unconditional kindness, hospitality, spirituality, cooperativeness with humility, unity and graciousness that touches the souls of others."[6] These powerful words indicate the infinite, without end. The well does not ever need to run dry. There is no shortage unless you choose there to be. We can all choose to embrace these feelings each day.

My father once told me that before my birth, my mom was nervous about me entering their lives. (Yes, I am the firstborn.) She was afraid because she felt she would not have enough love for him once I was born. He told me that he kindly told her, "Jean, love is not divided. It multiplies." Well said, Dad!

I believe this to be true: Love is endless. If you don't feel comfortable expressing your kindness in the words "love" or "aloha," then come up with your own word. It's not about the word, it's about how you treat others. You could call it "panda," if you like. Call it by the name you feel most comfortable using.

In his book *The Secrets and Mysteries of Hawaii*, Pila of Hawaii lists twelve symptoms that can help identify those who are afflicted with the spirit of aloha:[7]

1. "A tendency to think and act spontaneously rather from fears based on past experiences." *Wow, this hits on a lot of levels. Spontaneity is a key element to hospitality. Fear and living in the past do not promote the aloha spirit.*

2. "An unmistakable ability to enjoy each moment." *Yes!*

3. "Loss of interest in conflict." *Hospitality, like aloha, is drama-free.*

4. "Loss of interest in judging others." *It's not that difficult to give up judging; with impeccable hospitality you have no interest, no effort needed.*

5. "A loss of conflict." *With the judge permanently retired, conflict fades.*

6. "A loss of interest in interpreting the actions of others." *We continue to observe, without judgment.*

7. "Loss of ability to worry (this is a very serious symptom)." *Indeed! What will I do with all the extra worry-free time? Nice problem to have!*

8. "Frequent overwhelming episodes of appreciation." *A new way of seeing the world and your relationship with it.*

9. "Content feelings of connection with others and nature." *These connections can only get stronger with time.*

10. "Frequent attacks of smiling through the eyes of the heart
    (a dead giveaway for the carrier)." *This is getting very serious ... or
    is it sillyous?*

11. "Increased susceptibility to love extended by others as well as
    the uncontrollable urge to extend it." *Love multiplies.*

12. "An increased tendency to let things happen rather than make
    them happen (at this stage the disorder is untreatable)." *We
    cannot control our lives, but we can ride the wave with grace.*

Aloha, when translated literally, means "my life's breath goes with
you." What a great way to share yourself. It is the forming of two words:
alo, which means "to be with" and *ha*. Ha is defined as "breath, life,
the building block for Hawaiian spirituality." "As ritual, it connotes the
imparting of mystic powers through breathing on the recipient."[8]

Long before Western contact, Hawaiians had a deep connection to
the breath-life concept. The Hawaiians believed that *mana* was passed
through ha, our breath. Mana, in Hawaiian terms, is your power, your
traits or characteristics, your life purpose. If a strong connection is
made, the belief is that you can pass on your power to a recipient with
your breath. In Hawaiian rituals, the passing of mana was literally done
by breathing into another's mouth to transfer the power to help the sick
or injured, or from the dying elder to the successor who was to carry on
his or her work.

It is important to note that the breath is what gives our words power,
or mana, which is why we want to choose our words carefully. We want
to use our words (and breath) for good, to benefit ourselves and others.
Having integrity with how we use our breath is to live with purpose.

Ha is also the root of the word *haoli*. If you are a white boy like me
and enjoy spending time with locals, you will hear this word—I can

guarantee it. Haoli is the term for Westerners or white foreigners in Hawaii. Many consider it a derogatory term, and it is often intended as such. When it is used in a derogatory way, haoli means that you are not from here and therefore have less credibility; you are merely passing through. But my understanding is that its origin is more benign. It literally means "without breath." The story I was told is that it derives from the early days when the missionaries would come and teach the Hawaiians to love Jesus Christ, which they did. They loved hearing stories of this great man who lived years ago. And why not? They loved all life. However, the islanders were curious about these missionaries and how they could speak to the creator without doing any deep breathing first.

You see, the Hawaiians prepared and readied themselves before beginning a connection with God. By deep breathing and focusing, they prepared themselves for conversing with all spirits or ancestors. It was a purification ritual, and they considered it respectful and helpful. Focusing or cleansing the mind and heart was a necessary step. The missionaries, on the other hand, would walk in and begin praying without going through the preparation, literally praying with "no breath." We now know that deep breathing can calm us, connect us with ourselves, and help us focus—as the Hawaiians knew. Maybe if our missionary ancestors were paying better attention, they could have learned a thing or twelve from our island friends.

"Ha" is also in the name Hawaii. The way Pele of Hawaii tells the story is that when Captain Cook began exploring the islands, he asked what their land was called at each stop. At each stop, he got the same answer: Hawaii. What he didn't realize is that they were not speaking about the specific land that they were standing on; they were speaking in a much broader brushstroke. They did not live on the land; they lived with the earth: "Their life force dwells within the one Supreme Force of the Universe and rides upon the breath . . . That breath is called Ha . . . that life force is water [wai], which nurtures life, wai, epitomized with supreme causation known as ʻi.ʼ"[9] The Hawaiians were saying that they live and exist as children of the earth with their life-breath, and they knew and respected that water was the giver of life. They did not own or name the land they were on. They were living with the earth, the ocean, the streams, and receiving their gifts. They were amused that the white settlers could think that they could own the land by paying for it and building on it. That was absurd; the land could not be owned.

Other Hawaiian words created from the power around aloha are *kokua, kakau, kanaka makua,* and *hoʻokipa.* Kokua, at its simplest, means "to help." It can also translate to mean an extension of love, intention, a sacrifice to help others for their benefit and not for any personal gain. This can be done through kakau, or speaking the language of "we." It is not us and them; it is inclusive; we are in this together. While living on the Big Island, I was blessed with being on many kokua crews, groups of people helping to achieve an end goal of helping the community. Much aloha happens when you volunteer and use your time to help others.

Kanaka makua in Hawaiian translates to "an emotionally and mentally mature person." It is when a person of either sex leaves their childhood behind and is moving into responsible adulthood. But it is not based on age, as Mary Kawena Pukui explains: "A kanaka makua thinks . . . controls temper . . . is not scatterbrained . . . realizes that anger can cause *hihia* [entanglement, difficulty] [They are] sensible."[10] But this is only part of what it takes to be kanaka makua. Pukui explains further: "A Kanaka Makua is kind. He is thoughtful . . . senses the feelings of others."[11] And here is the icing on the cake: A true kanaka makua must possess the most prized attribute of Hawaiians—He must be hospitable. He must be warm and generous, giving and sharing always in a person-to-person way. He has outgrown the infantile grasping for all that he can get and holding on to what he has. He is generous of heart and free with his fortunes. In

Hawaiian hospitality, it is important to be generous and give freely. If someone invites you in for food, it is expected that you will accept—even if it is just a token bite. To refuse is considered stingy or stuck up. It is believed that a person who is unable to accept is also unable to give.

Ho'okipa is the closest word in Hawaiian for hospitality, and it expands on the concept. Here are some of the words that Rosa Say uses to define ho'okipa: "Welcome guests . . . even strangers with your spirit of Aloha, transcending the norm . . . the hospitality of complete giving. It defines a true art of unselfishly extending to others the best that we can give. In sharing our Ho'okipa with others, we gain our own joy and we invest in our own well-being."[12]

The act of giving permeates many other Indigenous and transplanted cultures. In his book *Lame Deer, Seeker of Visions*, John (Fire) Lame Deer tells us,

> "Before our white brothers came to civilize us . . . We had no locks or keys and so we had no thieves. If a man was so poor that he had no horse, tipi, or blanket, someone gave him these things. We were too civilized to place much value on personal belongings. We wanted to have things only in order to give them away. We had no money, and therefore a man's worth could not be measured by it. We had no written law, no attorneys or politicians, therefore we couldn't cheat. We really were in a bad way before the white man came."[13]

Imagine accumulating wealth only so that you can give it away to help others. Now *that* is generosity and great hospitality. It doesn't need to be about money; there are many ways to give. We can give of our time, and we can simply listen with no need to reply. This may be a great way of giving. Nearly all cultures have a version of giving as a cornerstone of great hospitality. A generosity of spirit is something that all of us can afford to lavish on others. It costs nothing and has the power to heal everything it touches. Another generous thing to do is to forgive and find strengths in others.

In Hawaiian, *lokahi* means that you search for a win-win, you compromise, you seek a positive outcome as your only goal. Many Native Americans also believed that fighting was not the path to winning, it was a last resort. When the first Europeans arrived, they found that the land was inhabited by a well-organized community comprised of five nations (Seneca, Oneida, Cayuga, Mohawk, Onondaga) collectively known as Haudenosaunee. Although these powerful tribes were experts in war, their government was not founded on strength of arms, but rather, on the art of peaceful reasoning.

Native Americans in general had a deep understanding of what it was to be free. They knew how to care and share with each other. They were respectful of each other, and each participated to enhance the health and well-being of the tribe. After living together for over sixty thousand years, they had figured out how best to live together. These five tribes knew that individually they were weaker and more vulnerable than when they were united.

One of my favorite stories comes from the way that the Mohawks dealt with interpersonal conflict. They had a ceremony that took place in the sweat lodge called Kill the Enemy. Sacred sweats were often done in groups to purify oneself or find answers. If an individual was angry with another tribe member or neighboring tribe, they would go through the process of changing the way they thought about their enemy. (If you can't change the world, change the world in you.) They would focus on what they admired about their enemy. My enemy has fast horses, my enemy is strong and rises early each morning before the sun, my enemy cares for his family and is a great hunter. My enemy is kind to others and supports his tribe. At the end of this ceremony, the enemy is no longer an adversary, but someone to be admired and potentially a friend. They have successfully killed the enemy because the enemy exists no more—they are in harmony, at peace.

The thing I like most about this process is that the Mohawk tribe, as individuals, were taking responsibility for themselves, personal accountability. They were not asking the enemy to change; they were taking personal responsibility for the way they thought and acted. They were showing empathy and power. They were coming from a place of strength. They had the power to change themselves; they were not a victim of their mind or ego. It is best to address all conflicts with empathy, forgiveness, and acceptance, no matter where the source.

Or as Henri J. M. Nouwen says in *Reaching Out: The Three Movements of the Spiritual Life,*

> "Hospitality means primarily the creation of free space where the stranger can enter and become a friend instead of an enemy. Hospitality is not to change people, but to offer them space where change can take place. It is not to bring men and women over to our side, but to offer freedom not disturbed by dividing lines."[14]

I love the idea of creating space for people to change as they desire. In this way you are not forcing anything on them, not boxing them in, just creating that space to make their own path. It is a powerful act that benefits the giver as well as the receiver.

In *The Courage to Teach*, Parker J. Palmer tells us,

> "Hospitality is always an act that benefits the host even more than the guest. The concept of hospitality arose in ancient

times when reciprocity was easier to see. In nomadic cultures, the food and shelter one gave to strangers yesterday is the food and shelter one hopes to receive from that stranger tomorrow. By offering hospitality, one participates in the endless reweaving of social fabric in which all can depend—thus, the gift of sustenance for the guest becomes a gift of hope for the host."[15]

It seems that our intention and hope are what truly drive our hospitality. Serge Kahili King, a Hawaiian shaman, teaches that energy flows where attention goes. If you intend to offer hospitality, then that is what you have. On the other hand, if your attention is always on the negative, as in focused on what you want, then you surround yourself with wanting and not having. It is better to believe that you have what you desire. It opens the door that wanting closes.

If you continually believe that you are without things that you need, you will remain in that state longer than if you believe that your needs will be met—or better yet, have already been met. If you were to wake up each morning thankful for all of the riches that you have and are about to receive, I wonder what could happen. I am guessing that you would find yourself in a happier and better place while noticing all the greatness that happens each day. That would be hospitality to yourself and could radiate to others.

I have great memories of fishing with my grandpa, Everett Johnson, who lived and owned the only hardware store in the small town of Zearing, Iowa. We would go over to Daken's Lake or to a rock quarry—commonly called the gravel pit—to fish for bass, bluegills, and sometimes bullheads. I was just learning how to cast using my new Zebco casting reel. I used to practice with a weight at one end of the line. I would cast it at fixed targets in my grandfather's side yard. I was getting pretty good at hitting targets and was thinking that with an open lake in front of me, I couldn't miss. I was full of confidence for my young age and proud of my shiny new lure that looked like a frog with short legs dangling at the end of my pole. My grandpa took us out to the gravel pit to try a new spot. Off to our left was a small pile of rocks about ten yards from shore. My grandfather warned me not to cast near the rock pile, as my lure could get snagged and I would lose it. I did not want to lose my new lure. All I could think was *Don't hit the rock pile, don't hit the rock pile, don't hit the rock pile.* I was looking directly at the rock pile and trying not to hit it, and guess what happened. Yes, I did a perfect cast, right on to the middle of the rock pile. I lost that lure on the very first cast. My grandpa couldn't believe it, and when he told my parents what happened, he said that I couldn't have hit it more dead center again if I tried. As it turned out, I was a pretty good caster, able to place lures just about anywhere I wanted, or more accurately, anywhere I was focused on.

This concept of looking where you want to go, or better yet not looking at where you do not want to end up, also applies to other things, like motorcycling. In cornering, you want to visualize your line, look where you want to go. If you do, you are most likely to follow that path with the aid of a little body English. If your eyes wander, you could too. If you round a corner with an obstruction, like a rock, don't look at the rock; look at the path around the rock. I have found that this is good advice, and when I have not followed it, I have found myself in some intense situations, needing to take emergency evasive actions. When you need to quickly make up for a lack of focus, it is never elegant. If I had not been distracted or let my eye wander, I would not have had that heart-stopping "Oh shit!" moment. Focusing on what you want to do and not on what you don't want to do seems like a good way to live life.

If we can continually focus on our path—what we would like for those around us and ourselves—versus what we don't want to happen, the route can go much smoother. For restaurants and other hospitality businesses, certain groups can be especially difficult to work with. A common dread is a celebratory group, specifically the bachelorette or bachelor parties. They go out to have a party, not a dining or tasting experience. When waiters or hospitalitarians discover they will be working with such a group, they tend to get a sinking feeling. They'll picture having to deal with guests who may want to be overserved alcohol, have the potential to be loud, and can be demanding. Sometimes getting everyone in one of these groups to listen and be on the same page can seem like herding cats.

Of course, this is not always the case, and for some, fear of serving large groups may seem cliché. But I have always believed that the reason things become cliché is because they are so often true. Using this example, if instead of dreading the event and trying to have minimum contact—meaning focusing on what you don't want to happen—you redoubled your effort to give the best service with incredible hospitality, it could turn out to be an incredible evening for everyone.

I have seen it happen, front and center. With a focus on a great outcome, *you* set the tone. Your energy is one of professionalism, empathy, intention, and having fun. If this attitude is applied, I have found that even the rowdiest groups will quickly fall into place or at least be responsive to coaxing. Getting into the mindset and focusing on great hospitality sets the tone for yourself first, and those around you can't resist following along (until they don't). Sometimes, you have to go back and pick up the stragglers. The tone is one of expectations and intention. If you are focused on what you intend to achieve, then others can follow you down that path. It does require leadership.

I have worked in restaurants and wineries where we have one or two staff members who specialize in these types of parties. They are good with larger groups because they have envisioned a successful path. They take control, and the guests love them by the end of the experience. They take the guests by the hand (figuratively) and guide them through an elegant experience.

On occasion, we all stumble off our game. We just don't feel it. When this happens, recognize it and redouble the intention. I have found that when you "fake it till you make it," you can often get yourself out of a funk and back in the game. You dig into your tool chest, and you stay on an unwavering path.

In restaurants, if you spend any time around the dishwashing station, you can get a real earful as waiters are dropping off plates. They will vent and complain about guests, but by the time they exit the kitchen door, they are all rosy and smiles because they are professionals.

My parents were social people. I was always fascinated watching them, my father in a suit and tie, my mother in a dress and 1960s jewelry, readying themselves to go out to dinner or hosting a dinner party at home. We held many parties in our home. I have memories of many guests over to our house at all hours of the day and evening. I can remember sleeping soundly to the chatter and laughter in the house when my parents were entertaining at night. The sound was very soothing. I remember observing that people were always great to each other as the guests were arriving, everyone was glad to see everyone else, and the event was always laughs and smiles.

After the last person left, however, I often heard another story. I heard about what was really happening behind the scenes (judgment), who said what or did what to whom, who was misbehaving.

The thing that I realized later in life is that we should all entertain this way more. It can be trying, but kindness has its own rewards. What if you (privately) didn't appreciate what someone said or did, or you disagreed politically, no big deal. What if you did your best to make them feel comfortable, and maybe by talking with them, you found out an amazing fact about their life. It was also surprising for me when the very person that my parents were complaining about, they later defended when someone else complained. It's a funny human trait, variable empathy.

Were my parents being fake? Maybe on the surface, but there was more going on underneath it all; people were connecting, doors had been opened, and maybe some had closed. To me, the main common denominator was twofold: 1) the hosts (my parents in this case) put on a smile and gave it a good try, and 2) they kept their smiles—sometimes through gritted teeth—and found a way through, same as a restaurant would. "Fake it until you make it" can get you over that hump. And as we have discovered, the only real hump to get over is *your* perception of that hump. Others are just being themselves. Since it's your hump, you might as well own it; you may learn something about how well that hump has been serving you.

Variable empathy also applies to how we view religions or other beliefs. Some view religion as building barriers, whereas others view religion as tearing down barriers. If we look closely at all religions, we see that they are open to interpretation by individuals *and* they have a common denominator. All religions or spiritual beliefs have the potential to set us up to take care of each other. It doesn't matter if you are of the Jewish faith, Christian, Taoist, Buddhist, Spiritualist, or Islamic, there are always strong teachings around hospitality and how you should behave toward strangers in a positive and gracious way.

One of my favorite messages around management—and good hospitality toward your staff—comes from Lao Tzu. I have fond memories of sitting on the Muni train in San Francisco on my way to work, trying to decipher the Tao Te Ching in the early 1990s. I must admit that most of the writing was beyond my understanding, but I had an overwhelming sense of "this seems right" as I read the passages. Occasionally, I was rewarded with some nuggets of clear understanding. At the time, I was in search of the meaning of enlightenment through reading Tao, Buddha, and pretty much anything I could get my hands on (including, oddly enough, Sir Arthur Conan Doyle's Sherlock Holmes). I felt that I was on a path, but I had no idea of where I was going, nor did I have a full realization of the depth of the pages in front of me. I was just assimilating for later contemplation, as it turns out. Broad brushstrokes. One passage rang clearer to me than the others in the Tao Te Ching. I have been carrying it with me ever since.

> *How does the sea become the king of all streams?*
> *Because it lies lower than they!*
> *Hence it is the king of all streams.*
> *Therefore, the Sage reigns over the people*
> *by humbling himself in speech;*
> *And leads the people by putting himself behind.*
> *Thus it is that when a Sage stands above the people,*
> *They do not feel the heaviness of his weight;*
> *And when he stands in front of the people,*
> *they do not feel hurt.*
> *Therefore all the world is glad to*
> *push him forward without getting tired of him.*
> *Just because he strives with nobody,*
> *Nobody can ever strive with him.*[16]

The last line from Lao Tzu for me is the most striking: "Just because he strives with nobody, Nobody can ever strive with him."[17] What's the saying? "It takes two to tango"? I love this because, once again, it wraps up much of what we have been saying and concentrates it into a single thought. Similar to "this too shall pass," it sets the tone that no one can affect you unless you choose to let them. *You* choose your path. *You* decide to react or not react to feedback. Happy feedback, join in! Negative feedback, choose not to react, and let it pass by or learn from it. Contemplate, yes. Empathize, yes. But if there is friction, *you* have created it by your own design and expectations. Sometimes friction can be a good thing; it can shape us into a better form. But there is always a choice. If I refuse to rise to the bait, does that make me happier and more grounded? Or does rising to the bait help me? Choose and learn.

As I read Lao Tzu's concepts in the 1990s, they spoke to me. As a manager and leader of people, I was looking for some big-picture concepts to fine-tune my style. At the time I was winging it, trying different things and experimenting with who I wanted to be as a manager. I still love these words as a management tool and meditate on them when I feel that I am veering off course. The thing is, leadership moments continuously come in and out of our lives.

In my view, these lessons also apply to our friends and family. Knowing when to lead, follow, or get out of the way is a tricky dance. Not talking over people, not giving unsolicited advice or standing in the way of their ambitions, can be difficult and an exercise in restraint or personal leadership. Our motivation should be focused on supporting those around us and in front of us, actively walking alongside them in their life adventures. We have a stake in others' lives. Supporting the people in our lives and celebrating their successes enriches our lives.

Danny Meyer agrees. He believes in supporting his staff, letting them make mistakes, and learning from them. It helps make his restaurant group one of the most successful in the country. He feels so strongly about supporting his staff that he makes that his number one priority over everything else. In chapter 11 of Danny Meyer's book *Setting the Table*, he confirms his philosophy when he lists the five main stakeholders "to whom we express our most caring hospitality and in whom we take our greatest interest."[18]

He listed them in priority:

1. Our employees
2. Our guests
3. Our community
4. Our suppliers
5. Our investors

He further states, "The interests of our own employees must be placed directly ahead of those of our guests because the only way we can consistently earn raves, win repeat business, and develop bonds of loyalty with our guests is first to ensure that our own team members feel jazzed about coming to work. Being jazzed is a combination of feeling motivated, enthusiastic, confident, proud, and at peace with the choice to work on our team."[19] He goes further to explain that in order to treat his investors well, all other pieces need to have a priority focus over them, meaning everyone else comes first. With this cycle of enlightened hospitality, I would wager that his investors have done very well financially.

He is humbling himself before his people in speech. He leads by putting himself behind. In this way, when he speaks, his staff does not feel hurt. They know that he cares enough to have created this nurturing environment. His staff literally pushes him and his company forward with great hospitality that starts at the top.

The cultures in Asia exhibit many of these concepts due to their national character. While in the West, the guest is expected to adapt to the wishes of the host, it is the reverse in many countries, including China. In China, the guests are treated with a great deal of respect and kindness. The guest is expected to do as they wish, and the host will adapt. To ask the guest to change their behavior can be considered rude. Even if the house is a nonsmoking house, if a guest asks if they may smoke, the host will offer an ashtray.

If you travel from the West to China, you can expect to be very well received. It is a point of national pride to receive visiting individuals as a guest of the nation, and each citizen may feel obligated to behave as the host representing the nation. As a Westerner, for example, you may be offered a seat on the train by an elderly, less able person so that you may sit. They are showing pride in hosting you in their country.

World travelers may tell you that Japan is a country that excels at service and hospitality. A high level of politeness may appear to be diminishing in some cultures, but it is on full display once you are in Japan. The ritualized courtesies of Japan seem to hearken back to an era of elevating the importance of showing your guests how important they are to you. Each country around the world has these rituals steeped in culture and tradition. Some have long-forgotten origins. We in the New World have deemed many of these rituals as fanciful but not practical, and we may feel that they take too much effort. We may occasionally experience these rituals as a quaint, cultural exhibition, or in some instances resuscitated back into life in this modern era.

In Japan, great hospitality is tied to the economic engine. Sociologists call it stakeholder capitalism. In the US, we have a shareholder capitalism. With stakeholder capitalism, the companies invest in the workers with training and spirit. In shareholder capitalism, the pressure is applied by the investors to make the most financially sound decisions and to make them happy. Danny Meyer has built his company on the principles and values of the Japanese culture by prioritizing the care of his staff.

The word *omotenashi* is recognized as the translation for hospitality in Japan. You can experience it everywhere—in hotels, restaurants, banks, and other businesses. It means caring for others, and the Japanese people are perfectionists when it comes to details. But there is a more profound word that takes us deeper into building a stronger connection with each other. It is an intense spirit of hospitality called *omoiyari*. It means that you are taking an active interest in other people and have a sensitivity to their needs (think enlightened hospitality). In Japan, omoiyari is ingrained in the upbringing and schooling of children. It is part of the social fabric and not considered separate, meaning that it is not turned on and off in people's daily lives.

Omoiyari is praised in schools. It is a way of thinking and being, connecting one's spirit with others and personal growth. It applies to oneself, connecting to your own self. It is a form of social intelligence, a way of looking at others without judgment, a conscious choice and effort to look at another person's perspective without judging them. Differences are accepted and appreciated without pigeonholing others as one thing or the other. There is no sense of right or wrong from someone else's perspective or for your own. Your perspective is not the correct one; it just belongs to you (for now). The ego is taken out of the equation, and empathy and understanding take its place.

The focus on action is the key component. When omoiyari is in action, neither I nor the other is the focus. It is not self-centered or altruistic. It is about the connection between the we; it is interdependent. It is focused on the other without losing oneself. When acting with omoiyari, we learn by seeing another's point of view; we can get outside of our own skin and deepen our understanding of others. With awareness of our own strengths, limitations, and appreciation for those of others, we can achieve positive change by adopting another's perspective without adapting and taking the perspective as our own. We can have understanding without embracing the ideas ourselves. This seems to me to put us in a place to be more engaged, or more precisely, the definition of the spirit of kakau and aloha.

When omoiyari is present, the most mundane interaction is transformed. Elevator rides become memorable, the process of leaving a restaurant becomes a highlight, a chance meeting in the park or business can change lives. It is a way of being; it is attention to intention. When I am a human being and not merely a human doing, I do not feel separate from anyone, any situation, or anything. The universe doesn't center around me; I am a very small piece of it. I was put here to learn to become a better human, and I am surrounded by knowledge and other beings like me. Every human and nonhuman interaction is laced with wealth.

The Indigenous people of the world learned from nature by watching birds and four-legged animals, and by speaking with plants and insects. They learned lessons that they could take with them for the betterment of life and the village. They were paying attention, they were not letting their environment get control of them; they were not victims. They were living their lives *with* the earth and its creatures.

Compared to our ancestors, we have many more distractions in the world today. In the age of electronics and rapid transportation, we are inundated with information. I know that I find myself getting drawn into it. The other day, I heard an interview on the radio. The man was telling the interviewer that technology was designed to serve us; we should not serve technology. If we are in fact serving technology, then we should be contemplating changes.

If you are drawn into devices and you find yourself missing time, you can stop. If you feel that you are merely walking through life separate from those around you, you can change your habits. The oxygen mask analogy can be applied here: You cannot take care of others effectively until you've taken care of yourself. What better way of doing this than disconnecting the device and connecting with the people around you. Disconnecting should not be considered an errand on your to-do list; it's a potential learning experience. The person before us is not simply another customer or guest; it is possibly a future friend or professional helper. It is situational awareness.

Awareness is also about adapting. If I am throwing a dinner party and I am meeting my girlfriend's parents for the first time, you can bet that I will have one eye on the door and one eye on the rest of the guests in anticipation of their arrival. Once they arrive, I will be paying her parents a great amount of attention to ensure that they are having an enjoyable time. After all, how many chances will I have to make a good first impression? If, on the other hand, I am having friends join me for a Super Bowl party, I may answer the door by leaning back on the couch and yelling, "Come on in!" Are these guests less important than my girlfriend's parents? My guess is that they are not less important, but a casual observer may not get that impression from my behavior. My old friends are surely more important, as I have known them and cherished their relationships for far longer. So why do I slacken my hospitality when they arrive? Is it the right thing to do? I have one behavior for my buddies, one behavior for my girlfriend's parents, one behavior for my boss, and yet another for my peers. Am I a bad person?

I feel that customizing the way you display your hospitality and personalizing it for each friend is perfectly acceptable and shows intent. When I go back to the Midwest and meet someone that I know, but not well, I am friendly and cordial. I will politely shake their hand and ask them how they've been. When I meet someone that I am close to and have been through a lot of shenanigans with, it will be a different greeting. The greeting will most likely contain insults, comments on clothing, hair loss, or weight change, and always an embrace. Does this mean that treating everyone kindly and extending beautiful courtesies could be considered rote or simply processing the experience? I think it depends on expectations and intent. Familiarity always plays a big role. Sometimes when I have expectations around a repeated experience—say, when I travel home or visit a familiar restaurant—I can feel happy that things have not changed much in my absence. Most people *love* consistency to a point. It is good to be able to depend on rituals, is it not? When I go to a restaurant and my favorite manager or waiter is not working that evening, I have to admit, I feel a little let down. I will stay and have a meal because I trust other staff members, but sometimes something is missing. It's about the specific connection. I could say that the same holds true for any constancy—saying hello to the person you see on your walk, or the warm cinnamon roll at your favorite café. Or it could be the same helpful face at the hardware store, bodega, or bank.

My favorite bank teller of all time was a young Asian woman who was always at the same Wells Fargo window at the foot of Market every day. I would go in each day to make the deposit for the restaurant or get change. Each day she was kind and helpful. As I left, I would say, "See you later, alligator." She would reply, "Goodbye." After a few weeks of this, I let her know that a more fun reply was to say, "After a while, crocodile." This became our new ritual. I would say, "See you later, alligator," and she would reply, "After a while, crocodile." I cherished that exchange. We weren't friends, and I had never seen her out from behind her counter, but I looked forward to going to the bank to see her smile and experience our exchange. It had become a ritual of connection. Eventually, she was moved to other responsibilities. I still went to the bank, but the previous joy was gone.

One day I was walking home and was getting ready to make my march uphill on Bush Street from Market, when over the ambient noise of Market Street I heard that familiar voice saying, "After a while, crocodile!" I spun around just in time to see her boarding a bus and waving back at me. My grin could not have been any larger. She didn't even know my name, but we had a connection, a fun ritual, and I will always remember her. My march uphill seemed easier that day.

Each one of us has familiar stories of connections with people who moments before were strangers. The bowing and gesturing that happens in Japan may seem unnecessary, but if you travel there often or live there, you have come to expect it. It has become part of your experience of the culture. You would certainly miss it if it was suddenly absent. It may be a ritual that is performed over and over again, but at one moment, even for just a second, it is meant only for you; it is your moment. At that moment, you can choose to connect and capture it or let it slip by; it's your choice.

Sometimes, it's the unsuspecting connections that truly take us by surprise. I was recently on a trip back to Iowa from California for a wedding that my cousin Mike Johnson was hosting for his daughter. I had chosen an audiobook called *Under the Big Black Sun* by John Doe and Tom DeSavia to listen to on the trip. It was narrated memories from the early days in the LA punk scene by people who were either playing in it, partying in it, or observing it. There was a revolution of sorts going on in the late '70s in many cities with certain young people rejecting what the mainstream was offering: arena rock, aka corporate rock, and Top 40 radio. I remember those exciting years of going to record stores in search of the newest music: the Ramones, the angry-sounding Clash, early Elvis Costello, UK Subs, X, The Pretenders, and others that made me think I could play bass back in 1977. Three to five notes, repeat, and done!

This audiobook touched on a personal happy note with me. As an alternative music lover in Iowa in the late '70s, I was part of a small but mighty group. The way that John Doe and others describe the early punks in LA reminded me of my roots as an early punk follower in Iowa. Yes, Iowa had its counterculture too, small as it was. As I listened while driving between the cornfields, I oddly began to draw parallels between how they described the beginning of their scene, my memories from the Iowa scene, and how I feel about great hospitality. I was connecting a series of seemingly unrelated dots again.

Maybe it was just my experience in the Midwest, but to me, punk rock was about heart, not talent or trappings. It was not about pleasing the masses. It was and is about connecting and expressing. Punk rock was a diverse unified force for me at the time. For many people, punk conjures up pictures of leather-clad, pierced, and tatted kids, anarchy, and violence. But not for me or others who were looking for something meaningful. At its core, it was quite a bit different than anything else we had experienced. And anyone who was there during the first incarnation would have to admit that it was an inclusive moment in time. If you wanted in, you were allowed in regardless of background, skin color, haircut, religion, wealth, or clothes. If you were there in the beginning, you would also remember the buzz, a torrent of energy, and a masterful three-minute song. It was poetry written at the tempo of a freight train, or pop with an intense rhythm or edge. You had come to expect something different, and you were ready to hang on for the ride. You knew that these artists would take you to a place of sweaty, writhing joy, a place that you couldn't return to until the next show. There was a passion that drove these musicians to do what they did each evening.

For me, great hospitality fits the spirit of the early, first-generation punks. It's about camaraderie, a sense of belonging, escaping the homogeneous, boring gray, a unifying force of discovery. It's stripped down and powerful. It isn't about how talented you are; anyone can join. Like the experience of the early punk bands, you know great hospitality is right when you feel it.

When you receive great hospitality, it speaks to you personally. You connect to the art form. Both punk and hospitality also have a sense of the "rules are meant to be broken." Great hospitality comes from going above and beyond, working with the tools you have at hand to make a unique, powerful, and special experience. It's about a purse left behind at the table being dropped off at the hotel where the guest is staying or catching a cab to the wine shop to pick up a special bottle of wine for a guest because you just sold the last bottle.

The person doling out this great hospitality is doing it from the heart. There is no blueprint. It's about expressing yourself. It's a state of mind and soul. It's about intent.

Great artists and hospitalitarians have a passion for plying their trade, and this passion is put on full display in its raw form when it's done from the heart. Great hospitality is stripped down, and the trappings are minimal or reduced. There are no soaring background vocals or great architecture necessary, no guitar solos. The quality of the china doesn't matter in hospitality, only the receiver and the artist, one on one, call and response, receiving the energy and giving it right back. You are not chasing the ratings, you are creating a new level, a new bar for those around you to reach. The ratings will come—or not. Punk, like great hospitality, is about sharing, having a good time, and not taking yourself too seriously. Like the Ramones, we accept you as one of us. Hospitality is so punk rock!

CHAPTER 5

Styles of Hospitality

When the going gets weird, the weird turn pro.

—HUNTER S. THOMPSON

THE EXPRESSION OF HOSPITALITY in all of its variants can be as diverse and vast as species in a rainforest. Cultures and individuals may not always agree on how to properly express empathy, respect, and love. The same holds true for receiving those efforts. Many romantic and platonic relationships have seen a fissure develop into a chasm based on the differences of how generosity, love, and hospitality are being delivered or received. Be it gifts, extra attention, touching, or a simple kindness, these acts can get great attention or go unnoticed because the person receiving them is not recognizing their intent.

Tina Turner has already asked what love has to do with it. If the "got to do with it" part is speaking about hospitality, then I think love has a lot to do with hospitality. It is love for your fellow man or woman. Are we showing love for strangers when making their life easy? You bet!

We can pigeonhole love as a singular entity or we can paint it full of colors with all of its complexity. It is all based on how you want to define the word, or more precisely, define your intent and actions around the word "love." For now, let's just say that love is caring for another human being. This care could be defined as being hospitable toward that person.

If we have this much difficulty with one word, it's easy to see how misunderstandings can take place. Meanings and intent can be misunderstood. If you were brought up in a family full of love and it was difficult to raise the money for a small gift, purchasing such a gift may be the way that you showed affection to each other. On the other hand, your friend may have been brought up with enough wealth that they had everything that they desired, except love and personal support. Under these circumstances, there could easily be a misunderstanding. A feeling may exist, (assuming) that one or the other is not delivering on the relationship. Gifts may mean nothing to one of the recipients, and full attention may not be exceptional to the other. Granted, this is an oversimplification, but I think you get the idea.

In China, an offering of food must be refused many times before the meaning is clear and the offering has ceased. It is expected that there will be a refusal on the first attempt, as the guest does not wish to appear greedy, so multiple offerings are made. To a Westerner, repeated offerings of the same item could be viewed as pushy or irritating. (If I wanted it, I would have said yes the first time.) The act of continued offerings is intended to show kindness and generosity. The intentions are pure, but there is a potential for a misunderstanding. Misunderstandings can happen to individuals from the same cultures or differing cultures. Depending on your history or family culture, you may expect that "everyone knows" how to care for another. Yet if you google "how to show love," the list is sizable and includes many different answers, such as "small weekly personalized gifts count more than rare splashy ones" and "make time, listen, and give affirmation."

I love my parents, but when they were alive, I felt that in the gift-giving department, they thought that more was better. Every Christmas, I would end up with items boxed and ready for me to pass on to the Salvation Army. I truly appreciated their efforts and never wanted to hurt their feelings, but it was sometimes a bit much. Was I being picky and hard to buy for? Perhaps, but I had an idea of what I needed and did not need, and while they were definitely boosting the economy, I felt that much of what I received could be appreciated by someone else more than me.

In a movie I was recently watching, there was an exchange between two characters in an uncomfortable situation. One was nervously talking on and on about how they were feeling, and the other was not saying a word. As the scene went on, I became more confused about where the talker was taking the scene, but I felt I knew exactly how the silent character felt. The words were getting in the way. Body language and facial expressions were more clear to me; I could have turned the sound off and it would not have made much difference. Words can be a nervous defense. I feel that they can also dilute what is really going on inside any of us unless the words are thoughtfully chosen. I guess my point here is that we express ourselves every day in nonverbal terms. I also feel that great hospitality and love can be expressed in a nonverbal way and have the same strong impact. If the recipient is paying attention, then no matter the words being used, the recipient will have a clear understanding of what is going on. It is always better, however, that the action matches the words for the most powerful impact. Then the recipient can truly feel cared for. On occasion, no words need to be spoken at all. The act of reaching for someone's hand speaks for itself.

As a front-of-the-house manager in restaurants and as an instructor at the Culinary Institute of America at Greystone, I would push my staff and students to find ways of delivering silent service. Of course, you needed to converse at the time of order-taking, but I felt that it was pretty much unnecessary after that. After all, our guests were not there to be entertained by us, and they certainly didn't need to be interrupted every time we approached the table. Anything that needed to happen at the table could be taken care of through moving into space and out of the space, with hand gestures and eye contact—no words necessary. In this way, we were delivering great service quietly and efficiently, which gave the impression of great hospitality without words. It was a professional touch that respected the guests' space, and it was good practice for these future chefs to pay attention to body language and not expect to be told what the guest wanted next. Everything that was needed was in place before it was needed; anything that was no longer needed was removed. It was a kinetic balancing act of organization—all action and few words. We were caring for our guests by doing and being, being present with our watchful eyes and doing what was needed to make their experience better—truly taking care of them.

The response from our guests' points of view was one of gratitude. Most did not remember any particular point of service, but the feeling was that everything got done. Some would voice their amazement. It was as if the staff was invisible. We had delivered invisible service as part of our hospitality. The guests simply experienced our service— not in an intrusive, obvious way, but omnipresent. Our service came to the forefront of the guests' experience only after it was over. It became memorable, *and* it improved our powers of observation. When we saw the host pick up the wine list, we were nearby to receive the selection. If we emptied a bottle of wine or the guest finished their drink, we merely needed to catch their eye and gesture to get a response. The experience was subliminally sublime. It was a seamless dance, and it was pretty darned cool.

From our perspective, how to achieve this seamless service was a challenging puzzle to solve. How to get the plate from the center of the table without interrupting the conversation. Consolidate the visits to the table, get support to perform a simultaneous clear, and refill waters at the same time. It was a dance, and it helped us to fine-tune our craft. Sometimes, words just get in the way.

In life, there are often ways to show that you care or to express your love for someone without words. Simply showing up is the ultimate expression of caring. Being there physically and being present emotionally for someone says so much. Listening or taking action and doing things to make someone's life easier also works. Making a cup of coffee in the morning and handing it to someone you care about sends a message. Making the bed first will send a positive message. Random surprises and support in ways that are personal say, "I am paying attention. I have you in my heart."

There is also one very important way to show someone that you care without uttering a single word. It is called forgiveness. Unlike Inigo Montoya, who declared that he was in the revenge business in *The Princess Bride*, hospitalitarians are not in the revenge business. We don't get even; we do what is right. In my experience, forgiveness happens in your body. It does not come from your brain and make its way out of your mouth. This holds true for forgiving yourself, too. Forgiveness begins at home. Forgive yourself often and always.

When the team did speak, we used phrases or replies that had meaning, integrity. We used words of affirmation. The idea was not to be rote. Phrases like "right away," "my pleasure," and "of course" were not to be repeated over and over. They were to be applied only when appropriate. Being creative with our replies based on reading the guest was much more fun and engaging. This customization helped to build the connection. It was us paying attention with intention.

Sometimes a guest and a server—or people in general—are simply not a good match. It is easy to misread someone; we can become too familiar or not familiar enough. When this happens, we adjust. We heighten our awareness and change it up. Observation and flexibility. Or as Neale Donald Walsch wrote in *Conversations with God*: "Increase your observational skills/See what is so/then do what works."[1]

In other words, what does this situation need now? What can I do to move things in the right direction, get things back on track? It may not be that easy or natural, and it can be a moving target depending on the person. They may have their own ideas about what would be considered great hospitality.

It is up to the individual hospitality giver to read the person across from them and make adjustments. But you have to get in there and try; it takes effort, and sometimes it's messy. You may not hit it out of the park, but you keep your eye on the ball and keep swinging in an authentic way. Since scientists say that 60 percent of language is nonverbal; it is up to us to pay attention to that 60 percent and adapt. We cannot rely on anyone to tell us what they want. They may not even know what they want. We need to observe, see what is going on, and then do what works.

I feel that when we miss these cues repeatedly, we begin to struggle as a business, friend, lover, and human. I combine these relationships because I believe that when it comes to how we treat each other, there should be no dividing line differentiating our business world from our personal lives. It is all about the human experience. Like the universe, which we are told is infinite, I believe that the human experience is also infinite. Like snowflakes, no two experiences are the same, and that's OK. Actually, it's better than OK; it's very exciting.

Can we draw a direct correlation between the amount of effort and attention that is directed into any relationship and its success? In physics, we learned that for every action there is an equal and opposite reaction. You may not be able to apply a scientific law to hospitality, but there will always be a reaction, even if not equal (and hopefully not opposite). Whether our actions are as simple as opening the door for someone with the result of them getting in line in front of you, making eye contact *and* smiling with a hello, or meeting someone at their hotel with a lost item, the amount of appreciation can be directly proportional to the effort.

Think about your conversations with a loved one. If you say, "I love you" at the end of every call, it may have a little impact after a certain amount of time, or maybe not. What if you forgot to say it one time; would that be awkward? If, however, you mix it up and personalize it based on the conversation you just had, it could have a bigger impact, as long as it is sincere. Sincerity is *always* key.

The important thing is that you are in sync and sincere with the person across from you. If you are out of sync, simply observe. Then adjust and see what works. Once you are in sync, run with it. It is about being in this together, the connection, the shared experience.

We've all had moments when someone says something that triggers us. It could be a shared positive experience or an inside joke. You catch your friend's eyes and realize you are both thinking the same thing, sharing the moment without a word. It could also be a negative trigger. Hopefully, the person across from you notices and cares enough to adjust or inquire.

These triggers and connections can be tougher to read with strangers, but they can still happen. When it comes to making a connection, there is no secret, consistent method, or line. Like the elusive perfect pickup line, nothing works well globally. There is rarely a shortcut to making connections unless both parties are ready to jump in together. It can take effort, but no matter how much effort it takes, the true professionals don't give up.

Hospitalitarians are notorious for doubling down and increasing the effort into "cracking the case." It's a "they will not leave until I get a positive reaction from them" kind of attitude. As you practice your art form, your bag of tricks becomes larger and more specialized. Sometimes, you have to dust off tools that you have not used in years to turn a guest or friend around. Be open to body language and ideas. Ask what the situation needs now.

Our second agreement commands that nothing anyone says will be taken personally. However, winning them over is personal. For us, failure is not an option. Hospitality as a practice shuns excuses. When hospitality fails miserably, it is not due to circumstances or the environment; it is due to heart. Whether you are the giver or receiver, some hearts are too timid to open fully. Hospitality thrives in the courageous.

What if human interaction is diminished by design? There seems to be a move in retail and restaurants to reduce human contact through technology. You can have anything delivered, even your groceries. No human contact necessary. We have also seen automat-style eating establishments pop up that are designed to have little or no human interaction whatsoever. You use an iPad to place your order, and your order arrives in a little cubby in a few short minutes. Yes, humans made your meal, but you didn't wait in line (unless it was to get on the iPad) or have to talk to anyone.

To my mind, these situations could be beneficial. For those who are in a hurry, on a long phone call, or don't want human contact, these could be perfect. A person could multitask on the way to a warm meal without being the jerk on the phone or skipping a meal.

Is the idea of hospitality built into these styles of pickup concepts? Is the owner filling a niche? Or is it cold and antiseptic? I think that depends on you. I feel the thought and effort that went into the concept was built around a need or at least a perceived need. That sounds like hospitality to me. And who knows, it could happen that two people who wanted a transaction free of human interaction could have a romantic interaction of their own. Weirder things have happened. Robots and artificial intelligence are coming into our lives to help make things more convenient. Domino's is experimenting with drones and robot pizza delivery. Ivy by Go Moment is a text-friendly AI that checks in with you at the time of check-in at hotels across the country. It can get theater tickets, reservations, drinks poolside, or a phone charger for you simply by requesting it by replying to its initial text. These cognitive hotels have the ability to give you better service through Ivy. They claim that Ivy can handle 90 percent of the requests without contacting a human and that all texts requiring human expertise are read within three minutes.

The theory behind these automated systems is not new to hospitality. I can remember having a three-ring binder (analog) that listed each of our regular customers and their likes and dislikes. When a reservation popped up with a familiar name, we would go to the binder to find out their favorite table, allergies, likes and dislikes, birthdays, and any other pertinent information. It is always impressive having a Manhattan show up at the table right after you've been seated because that is what you have always ordered. The Ritz-Carlton built a proprietary system called Mystique. They built it in-house with the early goal of noting five preferences for each guest. It was then their goal to perform at least three of these preferences on every subsequent visit to any Ritz-Carlton in the world. With Mystique in play, as a frequent guest of the Ritz-Carlton, you could be guaranteed a customized experience based on your previous desires anywhere in the world. This system has been greatly expanded from its earlier roots, but its intentions are still the same: building a seamless invisible system to help elevate the human experience.

These technological systems on their own may seem dry. As with the cell phone in your hand, it only takes on energy and life through your perception and how you choose to experience it. The system—no matter if it is pen and paper or a complex computer program—is merely that, a system. I believe that the human experience carries the warmth and wonder. It is the human that observes, communicates, and anticipates. The mechanics, or binary systems, are—and should be—invisible as a means to the end, the levers and systems that are hidden behind the curtain. How you choose to use the technology to enhance the connection is the key.

When face-to-face, our focus should be observation and reading the complex code of body language, inflections, and speech—literally reading the person in front of you. If, as stated, 60 percent of human communication is nonverbal, our ears are limited to 40 percent of the interpretation. Reading anyone requires listening with your eyes, heart, and ears. It is a complex code that requires all senses to decipher accurately.

Observing body language with groups can help us identify who is in charge or who is competing to be in charge and how best to move forward. Obviously, the person who grabs the wine list at a restaurant is the wine host, and this is where the attention should be directed for that purpose. The person trying to catch your eye could also want to play a leadership role with any group. With these groups or individuals, often facial expressions or body language such as folded arms or leaning forward can indicate what may be happening or an opportunity to make things better. It is also easy to misread body language or other expressions. Sometimes folded arms mean that the guest is cold; other times it can be read as detachment or defensiveness. It takes practice, but with attention and intention, you begin to get a sense of body language. With groups, the dynamic between the individuals matters. You are continually asking yourself, "Am I enhancing the moment or interrupting?"

When problems arise, you might ask yourself, "Do they just need to be heard, or are they asking for a solution or compensation? How long should I listen before going into problem-solving mode?" In my experience, many of us pull the trigger and launch into problem-solving way too quickly. It is always a good idea to use listening and observing skills as your default. Listening is the bedrock of great hospitality. If you are not actively listening and observing, then you are no longer truly engaged. If you are disengaged, others know it, and any efforts you make run the risk of being judged as disingenuous.

When you feel that you are not being heard, it can shape the way you feel about any relationship. Being heard is a fundamental need for all humans. When you feel that you are not heard, you feel diminished. Listening and truly hearing others is the purest form of hospitality. It's the "I care" without words. Listening helps people feel better about themselves. There's no action needed when you're listening.

As it turns out, listening and empathizing can relieve, and sometimes correct, the situation better than action unless, of course, they are asking for action. Once you decide to act, you need to fulfill your promise 100 percent or you will compound the problem and lose their trust.

Trust is the pot of gold, the integrity we all need around us. Without trust, everything unravels. Trust is also the bookend to any encounter. They came to you because they trusted you or wanted to give you the opportunity to be trusted. Your goal is to enhance that trust. It begins with listening and ends with a follow-up, touching base to be sure that the plan worked out the way you intended. Whether it is a personal friend who you have wronged, apologized to, and given some time or a guest who is with you for a short time at a retail shop, you should always follow up to be sure that they are happy with the outcome. Trust is the cornerstone of hospitality.

For businesses and managers of people, the key for overall successful service with hospitality is two-pronged. One prong is an investment
in training. The second prong is walking the talk. If you invest in your
staff, support them, and take training seriously, you will reap the
rewards. If you take shortcuts and cut your staff loose from training too
early, you will spend more time recovering, which could have been pre-
vented. Once your staff is trained and ready to perform, their eyes will
be on you. You have to walk the talk; you need to support them and be
flawless in your execution. There must be consistency. It is OK to make
mistakes. When we make mistakes, we identify the mistakes and use
them as a learning tool. Fess up when you mess up, both in business
and in life. If, on the other hand, you are a "do as I say and not as I do"
manager/person, then all of your efforts will have no potency.

Traditionally, the point of the spear overseeing the training and
delivery of service with hospitality was the role of the maître d'. His
or her job was to make sure that the staff was trained, everything was
in place (*mise en place*), and each evening would go swimmingly. They
knew the room, the staff, their clientele, and their needs intimately.
They often greeted multiple generations of families over the decades of
service. At least that is how it was.

I mourn the demise of the role of maître d'. The maître d' was the
director. The maître d' was the person you wanted to know and who
knew your needs. He or she was in charge of everything in the dining
room. They knew your favorite seat, your likes, and your dislikes. In
some hotels and restaurants, the maître d' served children who became
adults and served their children as they plied their trade over decades.
We in this industry have been lax in passing on this legacy.

I came in late, just at the end of the popularity of a good front-per-
son. In the '90s San Francisco, we would visit Luigi at Bix, Nick at the
Ritz, or Doug and Maureen at Postrio. It wasn't about the food, how

many stars it had, or even if it was popular, which they all were, of course. It was about who was running the room, the door, or working the room. It was about recognition, camaraderie, and magic.

You could walk in at the last minute and take your chances. There may not be a table for an hour, but they would find you a nook to hang out in, make sure that you had drinks, come by and catch up, and eventually find you a spot even if it was at the bar. You were flexible because you had surprised them with your visit. It was not about the meal; it was about the camaraderie.

It was a live show, and excitement was in the air. On occasion, we might be introduced to another couple who was also waiting for a table, and we might have been seated together if all was amicable. Then all that was needed was a table for four, instead of two tables of two. Everyone won. The effort was there, we were not processed, and you never knew what magic lay ahead. Anything could happen as long as you were open to it.

You only get one chance for a first impression. Some restaurants or businesses can be intimidating for guests if they have never been there before, especially when visiting a popular restaurant for the first time. It can be made even more awkward without a reservation. I read a study once that said that if a person enters an unfamiliar environment and is not greeted or directed within thirty seconds, the body will begin developing symptoms of stress. Heart rates will rise, and palms can begin to sweat. If I visit a business for the first time, what a relief it is to be greeted immediately with a smile and an offer to help. The greeting smooths the path and creates a seamless transition from street to seat.

What happens if I don't have a reservation and the restaurant looks packed? Some guests have the idea that if they slip the host cash, they may be able to move up on the waitlist or even get on a waitlist. While this may be common in many busy and popular restaurants, in the more disciplined establishments, this does not happen.

In effect, you are offering to buy their service and reduce another's service at the same time with cash. When hospitality is for sale, is it authentic hospitality (judging)? In more disciplined houses, this transaction will be refused based on the integrity of running a respectable door. However, if the hosts do a great job for you and you choose to tip them afterward as a thank you, it will be gladly accepted. Integrity is treating everyone as an important guest.

I read an article on one bar that has experienced this on an intense level. It is called Multnomah Whiskey Library in Portland, Oregon. You could expect long waits in a popular New York, Chicago, or Los Angeles eatery or cocktail hot spot, but you wouldn't expect a three-hour wait for a seat at a bar in the Pacific Northwest. This wait comes for two reasons. They are small (sixty-five seats), and they have chosen to sell memberships. If you are a member, you can make a reservation. If you are a walk-in, you may get a spot if a member is not taking it. For this type of business, the front or maître d' position is key. For this reason, they have hired a manager to oversee the reservations and seating. The key function for the owners, according to Alan Davis, is to empower the door. It is not easy to help people feel happy once they have waited for three hours. And I can imagine the bribes that they are turning down to protect their members are somewhat significant.

How do you feel once you have entered a business and receive no recognition? You try to get someone's attention, but they are on the phone or talking with another employee or guest or simply absent. All you want is to talk to someone and get your needs met. Well, if you ask me, I will quote Giovanni Scala, owner of Scala's Bistro, who is always ready to let you have an old Neapolitan saying. He is fond of saying, "The fish stinks at the head." Yes, it's the owner, the boss, the manager, whoever is empowered to make these decisions. He was also fond of saying, "When you are cooking fish, you keep one eye on the fish and one eye on the cat." There should always be an eye on the door.

While the maître d' position is still alive and well in hotels, it has not maintained its status in most new restaurants. For many, the spotlight has moved from a warm greeting as the first impression, to a smile and processing your reservation. It has become a transaction to get you to a table where, hopefully, the service and hospitality can begin. The focus on the maître d' position has been replaced by the celebrity chef, the prime location, and the architect's touch. These appear to be the components that drive guests to high-end restaurants lately.

For the most part, the position of maître d' has been taken over by the restaurant manager, who is now required to perform many business tasks that are not related to caring for the guest. The caring attendants of the past have been replaced with younger, good-looking hosts who are not steeped in this iconic tradition. Through no fault of their own, the host position is not often seen as a career opportunity or as a position to grow your vocation. It is presented as a stepping-stone, a lily pad to other things, or as income to get one through school. Hosts are often hired with little experience, and with the sole focus of keeping the dining room full and marching diners to their table. There seems to be little emphasis on making a connection; it's considered a transition and a transaction.

The maître d' position seems to be going the way of table-side preparations. Rare is table-side Caesar salad or flaming dessert. The once overarching specialist position has diminished in number, as expenses have needed to be cut. It is expensive to run a restaurant, and payroll can eat up 30 percent or more of the profits, so a manager/owner needs to wear many hats to be profitable. Dining rooms today are overseen by managers who double as food runners, bookkeepers, bussers, drink runners, and plumbers or electricians when needed.

I feel that to ignore the maître d' or strong front position is to lose that great initial impression and is akin to stepping over dimes to get to nickels. For some reason, we refuse to invest in a higher-paying and higher-performing maître d'-style person for our business, thus missing opportunities to make a great first impression and a strong connection for the guest. We want the guests who visit our businesses to have a strong connection; we want them to return visit after visit and become evangelists for the business. Not only is it good business sense, but it's also a lot more fun.

I know that there are places where these feelings are still generated in restaurants, retail, and offices. I feel confident that these jewels in the greeting experience will continue to spring up in various forms, for us and our children to enjoy. We need to seek them out and support them with our visits.

I invite you to seek out these establishments where they make that extra effort. Get to know who these hospitalitarians are so that you recognize the familiar face or faces. And through your visits they will begin to know you. Forge that relationship and heighten your dining or retail experience. You may find yourself saddened when these characters decide to move on or retire. But you will have great memories. After all, life is about change, and anchor establishments in our towns and cities change over time. But in establishments that invest in prioritizing the connection, this change seems less severe.

I call on all of us to support, celebrate, and frequent the businesses that give us consistency, camaraderie, and comfort. Spend your money with people who give you joy. Make the connection, and don't settle for a simple transaction. I know I'm a dreamer and sometimes romanticize the past, but I miss the singular role of the maître d', the specialist in hospitality. I also draw comfort in the fact that the role continues to live on in spirit within great hospitalitarians all over the world.

I know that the reason I am so passionate about the revival of the maître d' position is due to my enthusiasm for connectedness. On any given day or night in any given restaurant or haunt, who is facing forward? Who is responsible for seizing opportunities? Who is responsible for the staff's connection? Whether it's a hardware store, a hotel, a grocery store, or a bank, it helps to have that eye on the door, keeping attention tuned to the arriving and departing guest. We need to help make their transition smooth, easy, fun, and memorable.

Unfortunately, now we have lost a generation of mentoring. The mentors are still out there, and I am hopeful that they are active and become vocal so that we can multiply and amplify this key point in hospitality. We do not want the initial human experience to become the luxury good and available only for those who can afford it.

CHAPTER 6

Everyday Hospitality

May you live all the days of your life.

—JONATHAN SWIFT

I S GIVING GREAT HOSPITALITY a skill that you are born with, or do you learn it? Is it in your DNA, like your hair color or bone structure? Or is hospitality simply a tool, something that you rely on for work or networking and then put away? Or is it the opposite, something that you take out when around friends but have no use for at work? Is it something that you tend to take out only when needed? Is hospitality applied like makeup or removed from a hanger and slipped on like a suit? Or maybe it's a pin that you wear on your lapel all waking hours in the day. Maybe you put it on like your socks and shoes in the morning and take it off when it's time to get some rest.

It should be clear by now that I believe that if you practice hospitality every day, it can enrich your life on many levels. It can keep you focused, bring you back from memories that no longer serve you, and help eliminate future concerns. Practicing hospitality will bring you back into the lightness of living in the moment. It can manifest as the spirit of aloha or omoiyari—a continual flow of sending blessings into and receiving blessings from the universe. And when the rewards come back many-fold, it completes the circuit—a practice in perpetual motion.

Even though great hospitality can recharge your batteries with positive energy, good rest is an important part of this equation. The health benefits of eating well, getting rest, and exercising are vital. They are the three pillars, the tripod of a healthy life. With low energy, the effort that hospitality requires on a daily basis can be overwhelming. With high energy, the extra effort to make that connection is negligible. In fact, you may even look forward to it.

It is to your benefit to set yourself up each day to engage in great hospitality. Simply doing little things for yourself, such as making time to walk or ride your bike to work, if you can, adds to a full energy day. Getting an early morning workout in or stopping for a coffee, preferably with a friend, can make a big difference. If you are making breakfast for the kids before dropping them off for school, give yourself some "you" time before waking them up, or have everything done ahead of time so that you can sit and enjoy breakfast with them. Get their day off to a great connected beginning. If one of your kids is up and the others are still sleeping, have some one-on-one time with the one who is awake.

Volunteering your time with organizations that you believe in can also help put a spring in your step. I see people who volunteer their time to organizations and efforts to help others as hospitalitarians in action. They help the sick, build structures for people in need, and help feed those who cannot tend to themselves. They help us pass on gracefully, and they read to our children, care for our elderly, and literally spread kindness.

Managers and owners who attach their companies or businesses to organizations that benefit the community are not only giving to the community but also to their employees. No one can give their time to those who need it (kokua) without feeling the rewards themselves. Giving can affect each of us in profound ways. Hospitality is an honored craft, and it can also be contagious; when you receive it, you want to pass it on. It is the oxygen in the air that we breathe!

By practicing the guidelines discussed in the previous chapters (no easy feat), we can enrich our lives and give ourselves more vitality to find unique connections and help make someone's day. Brightening someone's day can be as simple as a morning hug, saying hello to a stranger, or stopping for a moment for a brief conversation. It can be as complex as putting together a treasure hunt for a friend's birthday or organizing and performing a formal dinner party. For it to have the most potent effect, however, your hospitality must be sincere, heartfelt, and with the intention focused on the other person. In this way, both you and the recipient are rewarded. You can't fake or manipulate great hospitality and have it be truly effective.

Every one of us has great friends or extended family who were once strangers. Before knowing them, we could have walked right by them in a crowd, but we took the time and effort to get to know them. That made all the difference. If we choose to view all humans in broader terms, each of us is joined by the family of the human race. We all have commonality. When you choose the path of hospitality, caring for your fellow man or woman becomes a new priority.

Face-to-face discussions, talking, and listening with empathy is where change is made. The stranger can then no longer be a stranger. When listening empathetically, it is possible to have rewarding experiences with someone on the opposite end of the political spectrum, a person with divergent religious views, or one with opposing core values. When you are face-to-face and listening empathetically, your hackles can recede. You can then connect with the person across from you. You can actually hear and perhaps even understand their perspective. You see them as human, not as a concept. You can genuinely build a connection with them even if you don't agree with what they say. Each of us wants to be seen and heard. We desire to be recognized as someone beyond our experiences and beliefs. We might be hard on the outside, but many of us are soft and mushy on the inside; we are complex by nature. It's when we get labeled, when our complexities are oversimplified and we are put in a box, that things can go poorly. Changes can be made in relationships between all people once we are open to the possibility. Changes can be made in a perspective when we are empathetic, when we share, listen, and are open. Changes can be made in your day and your life. It doesn't take much effort.

Sometimes, all it takes is a smile, a wave, or a salutation to make someone's day. And doing so makes for a great beginning and is a surprising nugget of gold. It sets a tone. It sets your tone. When I lived at 800 Bush Street in San Francisco, I had my way of setting the tone. I lived just down the hill from the Ritz-Carlton on Nob Hill. I would often venture uphill—out of my way—on my walk to work simply to experience entering through the doors of the Ritz-Carlton. On some days, I would wake up feeling lackluster. Stepping into the Ritz-Carlton set the tone. I would trudge up the hill toward the front set of doors and watch as the impeccably dressed doormen swung open both doors with warm greetings and a smile. As I entered, I would see the person behind the front desk catch my eye with a "good morning." I would receive more warm greetings as I proceeded through the hotel and out the door and down California Street. This little side excursion had the effect of setting my mood for delivering great hospitality. I received eye contact and a warm greeting from every staff member I encountered, and maybe some happy guests to boot. On my way down California Street, I could wave and say hello to everyone on the cable cars and others walking by.

Farther on my walk, near Market Street, I could usually find my favorite homeless guy. I have forgotten his name, and he wasn't actually homeless. He once told me that he lived in an inexpensive hotel, but he made his money at the base of California Street. One day he shared that he had just gotten married, and he and his new bride were sharing the room. He made his rent money by selling bookmarks that were simply made of plain white paper with a stamp of Jesus on it. Each stamp of Jesus was just a few inches tall on a cut strip of paper. I would converse with him for a minute or two on my way to work whenever he was there. I also purchased his bookmarks for 25 cents each. I had so many bookmarks that I still find them every so often in a box, book, or drawer, decades later.

One day, I noticed when he was no longer in his corner. I felt a sense of sadness, the same way I was sad when Chicago Joe was no longer selling his hot dogs on the southeast corner of Union Square. I enjoyed seeing him at his cart. He had the best pepper relish, which made his dogs great. He told me that he would get up before sunrise and make the relish fresh every day. One day, the stranger operating his cart at that same corner told me that Joe had sold his cart. When I asked, he also stated that he did not make pepper relish. I looked forward to my rituals, and I had an emotional connection with these two men. I hope that they both moved on to greener pastures and are happy and healthy today.

I liked these á la minute connections. I also feel that I do not have them as often as I once did. I am consciously trying to rectify this each day. I feel that my attention to the device in my pocket has a lot to do with it. I can get distracted and miss opportunities while I check an email or text. I try to keep my device hidden in my pocket as much as possible, but it's tough. Our devices seem to be there to connect us in so many ways, and yet are disconnecting us from our immediate environment. Someone once told me, "It used to be that the internet was an escape from the real world; now the real world is an escape from the internet."

Some cherish the anonymity of head down or eyes on a screen. They don't enjoy the small-town nosiness that others thrive on. Seeing people who recognize you in the grocery store and want to talk to you can be annoying for some. Other people being involved in your life and knowing what you are up to is the way that I grew up, but for some it's an irritation. Some would rather be in a room of strangers, each person isolated and doing their thing, keeping themselves to themselves. I feel this way when my batteries are low. I have no energy to converse.

On the other hand, many cherish connections. For these people, it is about a healthy balance, about having a great day with a cherry on top. They enjoy taking time off from the screen to look around, see what is happening, or listen to their child tell them about an exciting moment. They enjoy holding the door for people and striking up a conversation in line at the cafe or with people sitting next to them in the theater.

I once met the conductor of the San Francisco Opera while having a beer at a newly opened brewery. He was a stranger, and I just happened to be sitting next to him. I could have said nothing to him and bypassed our conversation. I was with a friend, and we could have kept to ourselves. But he seemed open somehow, so I took a chance. My friend and I learned a lot about him and the life of a conductor from our forty-minute chat. Random chance? Sure, or maybe not. Maybe just paying attention to my surroundings and getting a vibe.

Our surroundings are important, so we may as well pay attention. They are important for safety as well as making connections with others and within yourself. I could never wear earbuds or headphones when I went for my walkabouts in San Francisco. I felt I needed to be in touch with my surroundings. Forgetting the most basic reason for safety in a dense city or crossing roadways, I needed to experience what was happening around me on a cellular level. I loved the sounds of my city. There was life going on around me, and I needed to be connected to it. Connection is undeniably the hospitality superpower. I loved the sounds and smells—well, at least most of them.

I needed my situational awareness—the context—to feel connected to the moment and not miss a thing. I loved knowing that I had figured out how to afford to live in San Francisco for more than ten years. I once read about a survey that was taken regarding the friendliest cities in the US. San Francisco was always up there in the early 1990s. One of the measuring sticks was the time it took for someone to inquire if you needed directions once you opened a map on the street. (Remember folded maps?) At the time, it was a nanosecond in SF. We were proud of our city and wanted to show it off whenever possible. How could I miss out on any opportunity just because I wanted to hear the Pixies or the Sugarcubes once again on my Walkman?

Situational awareness has taken on a more specific meaning today. Bad things are happening in the world and to our neighborhoods. People are living in fear, and they are hypervigilant. This makes it hard to trust people, especially strangers. Awareness has become a defensive measure. We can no longer afford to be oblivious to our surroundings.

Couldn't we use those same techniques to help enhance our lives as well as protecting them? Kind of a glass-half-full attitude about our surroundings with an eye on the whole, on opportunities as well as concerns? We should always be aware of *everything* that is going on around us, not just the suspicious stuff. We don't need earbuds as a protective device or entertainment while enjoying public areas. Our senses protect and provide for us; why would we want to diminish that? And if you haven't noticed, the world around us is pretty entertaining when you are looking at it with awareness.

As we actively travel through our day with awareness, we are presented with opportunities. These opportunities come with choices. When we make choices with hospitality in mind, we make choices that are about helping others in a meaningful way. When we take action with intent, we recognize the individual. Recognizing another through our positive actions and intent is a handshake of sorts. Helping people in need is great, as is seeking out opportunities to put the icing on someone's cake. Try holding the door open for *everyone*. Before the elevator door closes, check to see if anyone is rushing to it. Offer to help an overwhelmed family at the airport; push their stroller for them to free their hands. Smile at a stranger (but don't be creepy; their situational awareness could escalate things). Do acts of kindness for the people you love. Do acts of kindness for people that you don't know. Make the effort, pay attention to the signposts, interpret to the best of your ability, be yourself, and take action. Seize the opportunities, take risks, make mistakes. Do the best you can each day. Each action you take has an effect; it all adds up and adds to the energy of those around you. You are paying forward; you are starting an avalanche of joy. You do affect people's lives!

I can remember an experience I had with my friend Beth. Beth liked Budweiser. Many of us spent our beer money at one of the best beer bars ever, The Toronado, on Haight Street in San Francisco. The Toronado was known worldwide for having an amazing beer list. It was and is Mecca for many beer quaffers. You could say that we were spoiled being able to walk to The Toronado and enjoy the best collection of local and world-class beers at that time. There was no Bud, Miller, Coors, Hamms, PBR, and the like on the beer list. Dave Keene, the owner, was not interested in the more pedestrian varieties of the barley beverage. He was trying to elevate the beer experience from the time he opened the doors in the late '80s. By the early '90s, he was a pioneer. But he kept a case of Budweiser around for Beth. Great hospitality, right?

Beth eventually moved away from San Francisco. Once she was gone, so was her Budweiser. Mission accomplished! Of course, she eventually returned for a visit. I can remember sitting there with her sister Maggie and my friend Melissa. Beth was kindly told that Dave had removed Bud from the menu because she had moved away. Instead of being upset, Beth was elated at the fact. She stated, "How sweet. Dave retired my beer!" Hospitality returned! It's not just paying attention and not taking things personally. It's tweaking your perspective as well, to share the love, share the experience, and share the hospitality with each other. It's about expanding on the relationship.

There are many benefits to expanding relationships. Beyond the practical benefit of strengthening a friendship, networking and promoting a strong, genuine, and sincere relationship can benefit your health and happiness. Relationships can stabilize emotional turmoil and behave as an anchor when you feel that you are drifting out to sea.

Having a relationship with a caretaker can aid them in understanding the complete picture of your well-being. It is important to have a strong bond and deep relationship with the people we select to care for our minds and bodies. I feel that we should carefully select our doctor, chiropractor, acupuncturist, therapist, or masseuse based on our connection to them. Try a few out, take them out for a spin. If you are not feeling a connection, try another one. Pick the one you connect with. Your mind and body are not mechanical; they're alive and they benefit from connections.

If you *are* a doctor, nurse, or other health professional, apply these efforts of practicing great hospitality. Make connections part of your practice/bedside manner. Isn't being sick or injured bad enough without having a grouchy, distant, or rushed caretaker? I can't help but think that there will be more open and candid conversations if the patient and caretaker stop thinking about each other as patient and caretaker and begin trying to connect as humans with unique needs. I know that I often feel "processed" when I am being treated by a medical professional, and it doesn't feel great.

I heard a great interview on the radio one day about a group of medical professionals with an unusual point of view. These behind-the-scenes players were taking their intention to another level. The team was in charge of setting up the trays that were destined for surgical procedures. The person being interviewed was telling the interviewer about how she thought deeply and with intention while setting up these trays. She and her coworkers felt strongly that these trays needed to be perfect; a person's life could be dependent on them. Some of these professionals admitted to praying for the person as they set up the essential tools that were intended to enhance their life. They had no idea if this person was man or woman, young or old, but they prayed with the intention for a good outcome. They knew that they would never meet that person, but they held them in their thoughts and heart nonetheless. I think that this is a great effort to make a remote connection. It was a practice in casting healing prayers with therapeutic intention to an unknown recipient.

I know that many medical professionals are rushed by their workload. I was told by a doctor that she had an average of fifteen minutes to spend with each patient to keep her schedule on time. If she went over, it was tough to recover. This sounds stressful. Maybe someday the priorities will change. After all, shouldn't there be hospitality in the hospital?

I feel that we need to stop looking at all businesses and lives as mere transactions and begin viewing these exchanges as the opportunity to connect. Viewing from a connection perspective and putting our money where our heart is could change our landscape. Good places would thrive, and disconnected places would either be raised up or wither. If we consider spending our hard-earned money with a connection in mind, where would we spend that money? Would you continue to fortify the establishments where all you received was a transaction? Or would you transfer your dollar to where you had a great connection? We want both the transaction and the connection, right? So why do we think that these two goals are at odds? I guess because sometimes places that make a connection can be difficult to frequent. Sometimes the connection is strong, but the service or product is not. And sometimes clean transactions can be easy but disconnected. It doesn't need to be one or the other. Maybe we should invest our time, energy, and dollars in a place that offers *both* a strong connection and positive transaction.

I have only purchased my tires from one place in the last fifteen years. Not because it's the best deal (it could be, I don't know) and not only because they always take great care of me, which they do. It's because Kevin at B&G Tires in Napa is visibly working hard to make sure that I, and everyone else, feel taken care of. He is the owner. He or a member of his team is on the phone in three rings. He directs his team on what is a current priority, and he changes priorities often based on what has the most urgency. He is high volume, and his team hustles because he is working beside them hustling as well. I have never driven my vehicle to B&G and not been greeted by Kevin or his son, Giovanni, within one minute, two at the most. Quite often, he or Giovanni is outside with another customer and saying hello to new arrivals. He is sure to let you know that he will be right with you, and when he gets with you, he is fully intent on your problem. He gives you options, gives you timing and expense, and he sticks to what he says. There's no BS, and he is always professional, friendly, and efficient. *That's* what I want in this transaction/connection. Is this feverish pace considered great hospitality? I feel well taken care of, so yes! He also has a five-star average on Yelp, so I am not alone. I have had this feeling of care at hardware stores, gas stations (outside the state of California), car washes, retail shops, and repair shops. Unfortunately, I infrequently feel this care at big box stores, which is a missed opportunity on their part.

In a professional setting, all it takes is recognition to get things off to a great start. Inside and outside of business, a simple smile goes a long way. Today, not all smiles are taken in a positive light. It can be difficult to trust the intention of some. But you should be able to trust yourself. There are many of us out in the world with good intentions, so heightened awareness helps to decipher these situations. You want to be able to trust yourself enough that you have confidence that you will not intentionally put yourself in any dangerous situation. The idea is to not let fear isolate us. Isolation shuts us down. Isolation and disconnecting are based on fear. This fear can often be manifest as rudeness when projected onto others. You should never feel entitled to be rude.

How you react to others can depend on your experiences and current situation. It can also be your location. One of the more memorable acts of kindness by a passerby that I received was as I was walking through the middle of Union Square in San Francisco. I was walking by a guy coming from the other direction, and he looked me straight in the eye and somewhat discreetly said, "Zipper!" Sure enough, my fly was down. I quickly and discreetly took care of it. Thanks, dude!

His act was sincere and had an element of kindness to it. Like spinach in your teeth, you want someone to point out if things are out of place. The person across from you has a different vantage point, like the beach ball theory. Others can help in a variety of ways, even if they are just walking by, if you let them in.

Again, these efforts need to be sincere. I felt that that stranger was sincere in helping me by pointing out that my fly was down, and he did it with a single word. Now *that's* efficient hospitality. Sometimes strangers treat us better than friends do. Have you ever felt a lack of sincerity by close friends when asking for a favor? We all have our boundaries, and they should be respected. Connections are strengthened with good, honest communication. It *is* about being impeccable with your word and not assuming. In order to make the best choices, you need to know where you stand, so ask questions. Knowing where you stand helps to eliminate misunderstandings. Sincerity, which is a form of truth, can play a big role in how acts of kindness are received as well as distributed. I believe that without sincerity and truth there is no hospitality; they are key ingredients.

Truth is important for trust. If we as hospitalitarians make things up, our lies will be exposed and reflect back on us. We should never fabricate anything, and always speak our truth. Even when it is embarrassing, the truth has fewer repercussions than a nontruth. It is always better to say, "I am not sure" or best yet, "Let me find out."

Sincerity and honesty are simple kindnesses that you can offer anyone. "They cost you nothing," as my friend David O'Malley is fond of saying. They are simple, and you don't have to pretend or put on an act. When you are sincere and honest, you will never get caught in a lie. Sincerity is the keeper of your freedom. There is a toast that I like very much. It was taught to me on the Big Island of Hawaii at a luau in a private home. It goes like this:

> *"Here is to lying, cheating, and stealing.*
> *Lying to save a friend,*
> *Cheating death,*
> *And stealing someone's heart."*

I love this toast because it is a good turn of phrase, but I am not sure I agree with it 100 percent. It's the lying to save a friend part I have trouble with. I am all for being faithful and loyal. I would definitely tell a white lie if I felt it could save someone from injustice, but I also believe that misrepresentation can backfire and make for misunderstandings. I guess there are a lot of gray areas in the human experience and no right answers for everyone, only what feels right for you. Once we decide to deviate from the truth, it is up to us to take responsibility for our words. This is why I think that honest sincerity is the simplest and best choice due to its simplicity. If you mean what you say, everything that you say will have more potency. Cheating death and stealing someone's heart is still at the top of my list, though!

When we recognize someone walking down the street and we greet them with a "How's it going?" are we being sincere, exhibiting our truth? Yes, if we really want to know and are willing to stop and take the time for a response. If we are merely saying it to be polite or out of habit, then maybe not so much. If we want to be impeccable with our words and speak with sincerity, then maybe we should not lean on catch phrases that we use over and over. We have the ability to be more creative and sincere, right? Maybe a more sincere greeting might be just a simple "Hi" or "Hey Jim" if you are not really interested in discussing how things are going. Or maybe just say, "Aloha!"

We learn quickly in restaurants not to ask questions simply out of politeness or habit that you do not really want to be answered. The question, "How are you doing tonight?" as a greeting can be a bomb-shell. It only takes one time for a guest to answer, "Well, I just buried my mother, and my brother and I aren't speaking anymore" or "I'd be better if I wasn't married to this jerk" to stop that question from being asked again.

In any case, it is not a sincere question when approaching a table or person for the first time in a professional capacity. As a professional hos-pitalitarian, it is of little interest how they were doing up to the time of their arrival. The primary interest of a great hospitalitarian is to ensure that the limited time that you have with these guests will free them from any burdens and expand on any happiness. A little background may be helpful, but the most important moment is now. A hospitalitarian is mainly interested in improving someone's day during the time spent with them, no matter how it has gone up to that point. By reading the friend or guest and making adjustments, you will find the right salve to remedy any previously negative situation.

Sincerity is always simpler than asking throwaway questions. It forces us to be engaged in reading the other person, and moreover engaged in the present moment, in the now. Sincerity helps us to establish integrity. It forces us to use our senses. It coaxes us into empathy and being *with* the person in front of us. Sincerity can also be a good way to deal with anger.

We all get angry. We should get angry; anger is part of the human experience. We can feel anger when we feel that an injustice has been done to another or ourselves. Frustration is a form of anger. These emotions are healthy to feel. It's what you do with the anger or frustration that makes the difference. If you are sincere and being impeccable with your words (and are not taking things personally), then you can speak to your anger and why you feel this way—preferably in a calm manner.

If you believe in the dichotomy "everything that is not based on love is based on fear," then anger is a form of that fear. You are reacting because you are afraid of something. The key here is to be aware of what you are feeling, and know that these are your feelings. It could be that your fear hasn't even happened yet, or perhaps it has happened in the past. If you deal with it within the now, it is easier to own it. If you own these feelings, then you can take responsibility for them. Once you take responsibility for these feelings, they are often better received by others. Your true message has more potency and a much better chance of being understood. You are acting with sincerity and integrity; you are behaving impeccably. Your goal here is to communicate while doing no harm. It's tough and it takes practice, but do your best.

I feel that great hospitality can come from this calmer place, especially when we can hold our words until we feel that we are speaking our truth with integrity and sincerity. It's hospitality to yourself and hospitality to others.

Think of a time in the past when you completely blew up. What were you feeling? Did someone make you angry? If you were able to calmly and respectfully address your feelings with another instead of blowing up, do you think that your message would have been better received? My guess is yes.

I was told once that repeatedly acting out in anger in the animal kingdom is a sign of mental illness. A wolf's community is its pack. The pack comes above all. If a member of the pack is continually snarling and fighting with others, the problem wolf will be banished.

Indigenous tribes would traditionally do the same thing with members who committed crimes against the village or did something outrageous based on anger. If it was extreme, they would be banished or be "invisible" to the tribe. Nothing is worse than not being seen. They would either live on their own or be forced to join another tribe. No one wants that angry person around. When anger has control of us, there is no honest, sincere communication happening; it is all based on reaction and lashing out.

If instead when we feel ourselves getting angry we take pause and examine our anger, we will be in a better place to use our words to express our most true feelings more calmly and clearly. Then others will more likely hear the intended message, and we will sincerely hold ourselves accountable for our feelings and actions. It helps to frame these moments in a way that expresses our realization that our anger is ours, and we have no intention of spreading it. We own it; it's ours to keep or discard.

If we can take the "us and them" out of the equation and exchange it for "we" or "us," nine out of ten times any anger or conflict can be greatly reduced, in my experience. It's not the staff vs. the guests, or teachers vs. parents, or county vs. landowner, or Republicans vs. Democrats. It's all of us in this together to find the best answer that works for us. It's about perspective; when we feel anger, we are focusing on our side of the beach ball only. To see the other colors and look at the whole, we need to listen to the other perspectives and communicate our perspective respectfully.

This can lead to better understanding and compromise. Compromise means finding a solution that works for all parties, the win-win. Compromise combined with understanding will mean that all members will be treated with empathy, dignity, and respect. This is not only killing the enemy, but also a healthier way to live.

Instead of focusing on our differences, focus on sameness. If you worked at it, you could find commonality with any form of life. If you are sitting on a park bench and watching the duck on the water, you could be thinking that you and the ducks both enjoy swimming in the water. You might admire the duck by thinking that it would be cool to have webbed feet and be able to fly. If you are lying in a field appreciating the plants around you, you may suddenly realize that you both need sunlight and are working in harmony by exchanging oxygen and carbon dioxide. You need each other to survive.

You could even connect with an elephant when you realize that you both need to watch where you are going so you don't injure someone or something. When we have compassion for different life and cultures, we are in a state of healing, and isolation is exchanged for connection. Everyone and everything that come in contact with compassion and connectivity are affected, whether they are conscious of it or not. Compassion is about breaking the cycle of action and reaction or walking in a fog. You teach others by demonstrating your compassion.

How we treat each other, and what we do to ensure a great experience each day, takes fortitude and resilience. It is a life habit. What am I going to do to ensure a great experience for myself today? What are one or two things that I want to work on today to make my experience great? I could help bag my groceries so that the line will move faster behind me. I could take the cart back to the cart rack. Maybe I just want to be more respectful of those around me, so I won't take that phone call while waiting in line. I will acknowledge my bartender on the first sip of this delicious cocktail he so carefully created. The person that I feel is irritating cannot irritate me today. If each day we choose one or two ways to help those around us, through connection, we could develop good habits to help make each day a little better for everyone, especially ourselves.

For me, my professional hospitality path began as a barman at 4th and Main in Cedar Falls, Iowa, in 1976. I was a daytime bartender and a nighttime DJ. Since then, I have worked in bars and restaurants with counter service, fine dining, more casual dining, Spanish tapas, French bistros, Italian eateries, outdoor cafes, a brewery, nightclubs, and pretty much everything in between.

Service styles in these esteemed establishments generally required multiple touches to fulfill expectations: the correct glass for each beverage, side plates, and specific utensils, or a specific sequence or placement on the table. There were many facets, and each had to be performed accurately and in a timely fashion for the service to be considered crisp and to set a tone. When the seating volume got intense, these points of service could cause stress. Servers, barmen, and busmen would all succumb to this stress, which could diminish their ability to give their guests great hospitality. It is quite difficult to stay engaged when you are not accustomed to juggling fire but are asked to do so. Your focus is merely on not getting burned.

Now that I no longer work in the restaurant business and I am more involved in the wine-tasting side, I find that the intensity of my job has diminished. I see far fewer touches, and accuracy has taken a wide berth. It is streamlined and straightforward for the frontline staff members in a tasting room. However, I have had an interesting observation. I have observed that even with service being more streamlined, staff members still get just as stressed out. Stress seems to be on a sliding scale. It is not actuated when a specific threshold has been crossed but is more relative and individual.

Working in a tasting room is generally slower paced with more time to spend connecting with your guests and delivering rewarding hospitality. In my specific situation, we have ninety minutes to pour five wines and tell the story for each wine. Each staff member has two tables, and we will get four turns on each table. That means that each station has to tell each of the five stories eight times over seven hours. I have found that some staff members get just as stressed as if they had to deliver and clear three courses to each of the guests. It seems stress is a moving target. And the last time I checked, stress is not fun.

This has underlined my already entrenched belief that stress is self-imposed. I know that this is not big news, but it is eye-opening when you experience it and see it happen in front of you. So, how do we reduce stress? There is no magic pill to swallow. Change is not easy, especially when it has momentum. When we seek inner change, it gets messy, it's difficult, and it takes courage. Inner change is not a coward's sport. It's complex, and it takes insight to unravel ourselves and open our hearts. There is no simple path.

When we seek to change ourselves within the context of hospitality, we expand our heart—our experience—so that stress and other negative factors fall away. We are then in the calming eye of the hurricane staying inside and protected from the high winds. With practice, we can grow calm, and the hurricane will diminish around us. Accepting ourselves and others as we are *right now* takes up room. It can be expansive and can push stress away.

Acceptance is big, not small. Accepting ourselves makes us bigger. Accepting others helps us grow. Small and simple is certainly safer, but also restrictive. If we want freedom, seek acceptance. Acceptance is also not passive; it's kinetic. Acceptance is a big embrace. Feel yourself wrapping your long, loving arms around yourself and others. This expansion will push out self-righteousness and ego and reduce the stress. As you embrace yourself and others, we do not need these burdensome, defensive, and weighty shields of protection. We are free. Free to have fun, free to follow our path and shed the things that no longer work for our well-being.

CHAPTER 7

The Bookend

*"The two most important days in your life are
the day you are born and the day you find out why."*

—MARK TWAIN

I T'S NOT OFTEN THAT an event happens in our lives that delights
and amazes us. Or at least not often enough. I can recall memories
of amazement when standing on the edge of the Grand Canyon
for the first time. I can also remember being delighted while hearing
details come together at a live show, the emotion welling up while
watching Olympic figure skating or hearing a story that has touched
me personally. I get a feeling that starts in the back of my neck and takes
over. These same feelings of wonderment and awe came about while
speaking with two young ladies named Talulah and Ruby Finkelstein
during an afternoon Zoom in late July 2020.

I had heard about these young hospitalitarians and their accomplishments over the past two years. I had admired their ideas and deeds
but had never spoken to them. I was a little nervous. I did not need to

be, however; they were charming and disarming and let me know that "there's no reason to be nervous, we're just two little girls."

While it is true that they were young, they were also a powerful example of community involvement. They are and were a positive influence locally, and they were already thinking globally.

This story begins in 2017 when the Finkelstein family took a family trip from their Napa Valley home to the Big Apple to visit a family friend named Laurie Philips. It was a trip that would redirect their lives.

As a transplant to New York, Laurie had become aware of what she saw as self-imposed isolation of her neighbors and fellow New Yorkers. They seemed to keep their eyes down as they went about their day, many with earphones in place. She also saw a noticeable lack of interaction among the people that she saw daily. She decided she wanted to do something about it, and she did.

She made a red oval button with the simple words "Be Kind" in white. Each day she wore the button as she headed out into the city. The button drew attention and compliments from people. It became an ice breaker that paid forward. Anyone who admired the button not only got a nice interaction but also got to keep the button. The arrangement was that they would also pass it along to the next person who commented on it.

While her older sister Talulah, age thirteen, was telling me the story, Ruby, age ten, chimed in, "We loved how our friend Laurie was passing out the Be Kind pins for everyone to be more interactive with each other." They both noticed how powerful these buttons were. New Yorkers—not known to be the friendliest of people—would stop what they were doing to compliment and comment on the button.

Once back home, and with the support of their parents, Holly and Judd, they started the Be Kind Napa movement. They said that while most people in Napa were pretty nice, they felt that there was room for more kindness. Spring forward to July of 2020, and after three years of their experience around kindness, I had the great fortune of spending an engaging forty-five minutes with these enthusiastic ladies. I was interested in hearing how things had evolved over the past few years. I was not disappointed, and I left the conversation with a lighter heart and was charged by their enthusiasm around their hospitality toward others.

I knew that Covid must have affected their endeavors, and that is where Talulah began: "Right now it is very important to be kind and do service for other people, especially because people are lonely and need more things while in quarantine." During the early days of Covid, these two young ladies discovered that the homeless shelter that was serving three meals a day was short of supplies, including eating utensils. They sent out emails and organized dozens of volunteers to help sanitize individual kits of forks, knives, spoons, and plates for the people who needed them at the shelter.

They also partnered with another youth-based service organization in Napa called the Gigg Group, headed by local youth leader Megan Dominici. The two groups, along with others in the community, put together packages of necessities for farm workers with Covid. Through their Be Kind Napa Facebook page, they got the word out, collected donations, and helped put these care packages of essentials together.

Talulah and Ruby also helped organize a group of kids to write letters to grocery workers and other essential workers to thank them for working during Covid.

At the time of our interview, they were putting together a video to send to the schools to create art and help them raise funds for a children's mural. Funds would be raised by selling a book of artwork submitted by the schools. The funds would be used to paint the selected children's mural in the Rail Arts District in Napa. In addition to helping individuals, their project was about inclusion, connection, and community.

When I asked what motivated them to put in all this hard work, Talulah spoke up: "We just see, notice, and observe what's going on. We aren't on social media, so our mom usually hears about it and then tells us." Ruby added, "Another reason why we are doing this is because we feel that being in quarantine is a privilege because some people with their jobs don't get to be in quarantine; they have to take care of other people, they don't get [to] sleep in their houses. We really want to appreciate those people by saying, 'You can do this, it will be gone soon . . . hopefully." Talulah added, "We are trying to do the most with what we can do right now." Ruby added, "Yeah, we want to show our appreciation." They both agreed that they are grateful. Being grateful, they told me, is their main motivation during the quarantine. They also informed me that it is not religious or political. It's "just to be kind."

Their army of kindness consists of a core group of kids called the Kindness Kids. Pre-Covid, these Kindness Kids met once a month as a group. They would come together with ideas and make decisions as a group for the next project that they agreed to pursue. This included kids of all ages and even a few adult friends who liked to attend the meetings. Ruby told me, "We named it Kindness Kids because we wanted to inspire more of our youth leaders to be kind." "And get involved with the community," Talulah added.

Wearing the button and their other efforts have made them new friends over the years, have created great conversations, and have even brought tears. One way that they inspire youth in the community is by speaking at schools and describing how the school can get involved in community service. They also like to work with kids who are getting bullied. Talulah told me, "We speak about not judging other people, letting other kids know it's OK to be who you are."

Besides working on larger projects like a coat drive, the Kindness Kids regularly help to collect gifts and have even sponsored birthday parties for homeless kids. They have a great relationship with businesses that can offer ice cream, treats, and a space to hold the event. What a difference that could make in a kid's life.

I was eager to find out how forming their organization and helping the community had changed the two of them over the past few years. Ruby told me that both she and Talulah were once bullied at their school and, yes, they would stand up for themselves, but they didn't have much experience with that. "I think that Be Kind has really changed me," Ruby said, "and learning how to stand up for yourself by not being mean to that other person, by just telling them that that was not OK. It's also changed me to be a more sympathetic person, and I feel I have more empathy since this started. I feel I have more experience in putting myself in others' shoes and helping people." Talulah added, "Before, I didn't really do much with the community, I was more focused on sports, which I still do, but I also now like helping others. Because of Be Kind I can now be kinder to others, do community service. I've also done leadership camps; I've learned a lot."

Ruby added, "If a person is not the nicest to you, you still have to be kind to them. You just have to make sure wherever you go, you just have to be kind. Treat people with respect and kindness. Make your day kind." To this, Talulah and her dad applauded in appreciation.

I knew that they must have had a number of great moments in their young lives, so I had to ask. "Last year, we went on a California road trip to Sacramento to see the capitol building," Talulah began. "My dad had set up the tour with a tour guide. Our guide was very grumpy. She lost us . . . on a tour! She left us in the other room and kept going. And it was just us on the tour!" Ruby interjected: "She called herself the grumpiest person in the capitol." Talulah continued: "It was awful, we just wanted to get out of there. We didn't even want to finish the tour. We were all wearing Be Kind pins because we tried to wear them everywhere. She was like, 'What are you wearing?' and we said, 'You can have it!' Because that's what you have to do, it's a rule. Then she's like, 'For me-e-e-e?' And she just changed, I swear! Then she gave us her pin. It was a little snowman. It was so cute. Then she started talking to us. She said, 'I'm so sorry, I've had this awful leg pain.' Then she took us to all these special places just because we gave her that pin. Then we didn't want to leave, she [started] introducing us to people in the hallway as the girls that started Be Kind." I found this to be a great example of the powers of hospitality with kindness.

Ruby added: "The main thing about that story was that she said that she used to be a janitor here and wanted to be a tour guide. She said, 'I got this job because I was kind, and then the pain started bothering me, and I grew grumpy.' Then we gave her the pin, and she turned kind again."

"I swear I think there were two different tour guides that day," Talulah told me emphatically. Judd, their dad, agreed. He said it was a transformation like he'd never seen.

Ruby had another standout moment: "When the first Be Kind event [a parade with homemade signs with words of kindness] started, I was amazed at how many people came. It really felt powerful at the moment when people started to flood in with their Signs of Kindness, and I just started feeling amazed that so many people in our community were paying attention to the kindness that we need, and the power of kindness . . . It's not for us! The Be Kind event is not for us. Sure, it's our organization that's doing this, but it's to motivate people to be kind and to stretch their personalities to helping someone once a day." What a worthy goal!

A young girl in Chicago was motivated after hearing of these ladies and seeing what they were able to accomplish. She was also having problems at school and wasn't sure how to handle them. She called the Finkelsteins and asked how she could organize an event in Chicago after hearing about the Napa events. And she did it! Now Chicago has an annual Be Kind event.

Others have noticed as well. Judd says that they have been the recipient of a proclamation from the city board of supervisors declaring a Be Kind Day, a key to the city, and recognition from the US Congress. They were both a little embarrassed at their father's bragging. Over Talulah's objections to her dad, Ruby said, "We need to be humble." They are humble in their attitude, but not in their ambitions. As they told me that day, they are not content with Be Kind Napa; they are looking for a Be Kind World. *That* would be awesome!

Every day is made of choices; every minute is a choice. These ladies have made their choices. They choose how to spend their time, how to act, how to look at their lives, and their roles in the lives of others. They see a community, and they have *chosen* to draw that community together. It's a powerful example.

If we could follow Talulah and Ruby's example as well as the principles in the previous chapters, maybe our lives would be enriched and less stressful. New avenues could open to adventures and opportunities. Life could be more fun, more playful, less serious.

Striving to follow these principles takes effort—and it's not about cleverness; it's actually anti-clever. It's sincerity, support, trust, kindness. It's not about manipulating, it's more about thriving together. It's letting the people be who they are without judgment. We are not in the business to change people; people can change on their own or not. We merely open the door for them. The most permanent changes are from within anyway. One good way to help others help themselves is to be a good example. Well played, Talulah and Ruby!

Helping people can manifest in many ways, and the biggest common denominator is—you guessed it—connection. Connecting the dots is its own art form. As you may have surmised in the previous chapters, I have enjoyed reading the stories of Sherlock Holmes over the years. I love the character's ability to decouple the facts from the ambient noise. I have read the stories, watched the various movies, and listened to the radio programs with Basil Rathbone and Nigel Bruce. I enjoy his process. He connects things in a way that makes sense in the end, discards what doesn't fit, and creates a narrative that includes the facts and eliminates suppositions that don't work. It's observation and connecting the dots that drives the narrative, not the narrative (with assumptions) driving the narrative. *And* he operates equally well in the lawful world and the criminal world (no judgment).

Within the hospitality dialogue, we also examine the facts. The energy, words, and body language tell the story. We engage in an authentic way that solves the puzzle or keeps the game afoot. It is a realization that initial impressions can be quite false. And the only way to get to the truth is through observation, investigation, and discovery. It's about asking the right questions, and it may also require a magnifying glass . . . of sorts.

In the late 1990s, I sat on a panel of managers working in a hotel group. The goal of the panel was to attempt to figure out the value differences between the X generation and the Y generation. We wanted to assess how best to hire, care for, and motivate these generations that were coming of age. We were told by experts that these generations had different values. These meetings were set for one day a week. After several weeks, I felt that we were getting nowhere. We had a working list of how we could adapt our culture to better support the generation that was coming into the workforce, but no plan was forthcoming.

Being a firm believer that the more complex a problem is, the more it points to the simplest solution, I sat down and wrote an email to the president of the company who was spearheading these meetings. In the letter, I told her that if each of us focused on spending time with staff in a more personal and meaningful way, we would get to know the individual better on a personal level. We would learn their likes and dislikes. This seemed universal to me and not generation dependent, and each person would feel supported and cared for. That could be our new culture: universal care for each other. It would help build longevity and reduce turnover.

This was not me being a smarty-pants or a know-it-all sage. This was me looking for a common distilled link that would join us all. I had less belief that we were different than I had in the belief that we all had commonality. I also stated that if she wanted me to continue coming in for the panel discussions, I would be happy to, but this was my suggested solution.

I never heard from anyone regarding my thoughts. Two years later, I was working at Hualalai Resort on the Big Island, and one of the requirements of each manager was to talk story (slang for sharing personal thoughts) with the employees, to spend time talking with each staff member for at least thirty minutes every month about personal, nonwork things. Believe me when I tell you, if I missed someone and the month was ready to end, they tracked me down. It had great value for everyone. By spending meaningful time with the people whom we worked with, we were telling them that they mattered. And I felt joy that the time they spent with me was important to them. Together we were enriching each other's lives and treating each other with aloha.

The tools and thoughts discussed in this book require more than agreement; they require commitment. We need commitment behind the passion. Passion is impotent when there is no commitment. You may agree with everything written about hospitality, but unless you commit to changing yourself and making an effort each day, you will not be successful. I have known wonderful artists, musicians, and designers over the past few decades. So much talent, but—unfortunately too often—light on the commitment. These talented individuals had great ideas and talent, but their talent and ideas never saw the light of day because they were not committed to making them accessible. Commitment is action; it is the skeleton that supports the flesh and enables us to move forward. Commitment to practicing and pursuing the source, the root of what it is that drives you, is the only way you will be able to express who you truly are.

Commitment is about tossing aside trappings or distractions that don't serve us. Commitment can come as an insatiable thirst for information and immersion, with action. Commitment seems to have consistency at its core and stretching boundaries in its path. Consistency does not always look the same. It can change and evolve. Commitment is the endeavor to find the essence, the commonality, getting to the truth—your truth, no matter the outcome. The truth is pure and can be complex. The truth will appear to be superficially complex but has simplicity at its core. Just like one of Sherlock's solutions.

It's a feedback loop. Try something, get feedback, adjust, and try again, get feedback, repeat. Feedback can come in various forms: results, impressions, body language, or observation. Of course, this is all based on our current interpretation and degree of connection. This can be fun, a game of sorts. It can be effortless because *we* are not judging anyone or ourselves; we are immersed in the jet stream of life; we are along for the ride.

Whether you are winning or losing, it's all a perspective. One person's fun is another's boredom or fear. My grandfather told me several times in my life, "If you enjoy what you are doing for a living, you will never have to work a day in your life." Wise words, right? Even if he was paraphrasing Mr. Carnegie. If you enjoy what you do each day, then it's not *really* like going to work, and it can be fun. By the way, how did work get such a bad rap anyway?

I can't help but believe that if we follow some of the ideas, principles, and practices outlined by the previously mentioned masters and the two little girls above, we will have much richer lives. This information has always been available to us; it's not new. It is just a matter of taking this knowledge and wrapping it into a unique package that works for you. If it's *fun*, it *works* better. See how we twisted that around?

Thus far I have taken you through the tangled thicket of stories, philosophies, and teaching in a somewhat rambling way. Most of us like a tidy little package that we can refer to or keep on a refrigerator magnet to reference each time we go for a snack. It was not my intention of providing this fast food. However, if I were to blend aloha with Neale Donald Walsch, Eckhart Tolle, and don Miguel Ruiz and take a comb to it, it could untangle like this:

By living in the now, you will
Increase your observation skills
See what is (really) so
Then do what works:

- You are impeccable with your word
- You don't take anything personally
- You don't make assumptions, and
- You always do your best

We will then have an outpouring of aloha spirit (empathy and compassion), and most of all, we will build *trust*.

In the end, as a business or as an individual, we can distill the complexities to one simple word: trust. Trust is the end game; it's what we wish for. We will always make mistakes; it's how we grow. It is how we recover from these mistakes that builds trust. I feel that I have more trust in a person or business that has made a mistake with me and recovered gracefully—or at least with sincere effort—than I do with a person or business that has always seemed flawless. You are never sure of the true mettle of a person or a business when they appear to be a Mary Poppins and "practically perfect in every way." Recovering from mistakes will exercise all the tools in your hospitality tool chest, and the final structure of trust will be worth all efforts.

Trust is built over time. However, recovery can happen anytime. I believe that individuals and businesses should be pushing themselves by taking risks to be better each day. If we never take risks, we will not become as familiar with failure. With no risk, no failure, we will not enjoy the opportunity to fine-tune our recovery skills. Without practice, when we eventually fail, it will be more awkward. My hat is off to those who take chances, fail, and recover gracefully. These are the Olympic athletes of hospitality. I wish to be more like you.

Olympic athletes need to overcome more than just failure. Their training and discipline require that they strengthen themselves, building endurance and flexibility. With hospitalitarians (I wonder if we could make this an Olympic sport?), the strengths are the tools, endurance is the practice of living in the now, and the flexibility has to do with being more open.

In her book *Radical Hospitality*, Lonni Collins Pratt says, "The real question is not how dangerous that stranger is. The real question is, 'How dangerous will I become if I don't learn to be more open?'"[1] Closing yourself off from opportunities is dangerous, and the danger is to yourself. It's a choice, your choice. How do you want to live your life—protected from the elements like a bud, or open and glorious like a flower?

Being open means being secure and fearless while doing no harm. In your journey, you will be subjected to every slice of humanity and experience. You never know what's around the corner, but if you are open, you are ready to honor the experience. This can be exciting and scary but ultimately rewarding. In the hospitality industry, we learn that the guest is *not always* right, but they are *always* our guest—until they are not.

If a tree comes crashing down in the woods and you are nearby, it can be frightening. I've had it happen to me; it's loud and intense. People can be like that too. At the time that the tree fell while I was hiking in Muir Woods, I asked myself, if I had been on a different part of the trail, could it have struck me? In truth, I felt that I could have avoided it. It took a long time to come completely down with all the other trees around. Close calls happen in life too, and a common reaction is to close down. That can be a dangerous move for any of us. Much better to heighten the awareness, face the opportunities, and sidestep them when necessary in a fearless way.

What if that same tree had fallen and no one was around? Would it have made a noise? Hospitality asks this same philosophical question. If I am not open and connecting with those around me, is my presence felt? Am I contributing to this moment, or am I standing by silently, waiting for this moment to pass? We all need moments of downtime, detached and behaving like a piece of furniture. However, in my opinion, disengaged is not the recommended way to spend your day. How can I enjoy what the wilderness of humanity has to offer if I am not open and engaged?

We grow personally through openness and connection with others. As we rub up against each other on any given day, we get charmed, annoyed, and bored. These feelings are not about the other, as we have discovered; they are about us. As long as we focus on the individual in front of us and live in the moment, the judgment can begin to slide away and we will begin to see another person with human needs, strengths, and weaknesses.

Hospitality is part of a healthy and balanced life. It is within all of us to expand our experiences by delivering and receiving hospitality. The delivery of great hospitality is the antidote to loneliness. It has bravery at its core. It is about putting yourself out there, taking risks, falling occasionally, brushing yourself off, and healing your soul. In fact, it can feel like a contact sport at times as you deflect a multitude of excuses with intention. It's not for everybody, but if you have intent, hospitality can be learned and taught. For these reasons, I disagree with the idea put forth by many managers when they tell me that hospitality cannot be taught. Many believe that you can teach service skills, but not hospitality. With desire I have seen young awkward staff members become graceful swans escorting diners to their tables more elegantly than I ever could. It can be taught.

When you are going through a stretch when you are not feeling it, or feel that you need to recharge your hospitality battery, find someone whom you respect and admire for their hospitality. Spend time with them, observe them, and listen and learn from them. Be inspired by them. Observe from afar, ask questions, and find your perspective on why and how the practice of hospitality can enrich your life. Each of us has a path; yours needs to be authentic to you. If you are fully committed, hospitality will slowly become who you are. Projecting hospitality will begin to encompass all your simplicities and complexities, your humor, your philosophy. It can get messy, but messes can be cleaned up, once you have the intention to do so.

In discovering your true self, you are inviting others to experience their true selves. When two people engage, they have the opportunity to see another perspective. Hospitality is about seeing the best in people or the worst without judgment. Without the judge getting in the way, the joy comes forward within that connection. In this way, we are in humble service to each other.

Many of us declare that we are in the hospitality business. When it comes right down to it, some of us are and some of us aren't. Any of us can say that we are in the hotel business, the restaurant business, or the resort, culinary arts, or catering business. But if you declare that you are in the hospitality business, you better be in the business of hospitality. With this in mind, bankers, insurance agents, and retail could all be in the hospitality business.

Unlike service-oriented businesses, hospitality is not just doing; it is about becoming. It's something that we can lean into. It has depth, meaning. It's sticky, and it's enriched by emotion. When we are in it, time stretches and contracts. It's about stretching ourselves through patience and acceptance. Not passive acceptance, but a kinetic embrace. Embracing people of different walks of life, different theologies, different political beliefs. It's about celebrating our differences, even if we don't understand them. It's a leap of faith, curiosity. It's raw kindness.

If you are a business owner, you may ask yourself, will my bottom line grow with great hospitality? The bottom line is that *you* will grow as a person, as an individual, and your business and people around you will grow with you. You will also build trust. Hospitality is a unifying force, and it will attract people like a moth to a porch light. Hospitality is not just something you *can* do. Connection and self-reflection are things you *must* do, today and every day.

With practice, you can be the teacher and lead by example. You can reset yourself, get back to basics, embrace the complexities, and distill them to simplicity. So maybe, instead of propelling ourselves forward without direction, searching for the next big opportunity to make us successful, we are now searching within and grounding ourselves in universal truths. Those that came before us have much to teach us about many concepts, including graceful hospitality. There are exposed jewels ready to be mined, if we open ourselves to seeing them. Be it the written word or the person standing next to you, seek out this knowledge, another prospective. We can be the new tribe, a tribe of heretics casting verbal lies over total strangers—strangers who may not remain that way for long. Strangers who change our lives for the better. It happens all the time.

Our new tribe of hospitalitarians is upbeat, even when others are trying to beat us down. It's a "kicking against the (negative) bricks" kind of attitude. Not Pollyannaish, being cheerful for the sake of being cheerful, but actively engaging in our surroundings and raising it up. It's a "you can't pull me into your quagmire" fighting warrior/adventurer attitude. It's a positive life force, and with enough participants, it can become a movement. A movement based on affirmation and trust.

Hospitality is about finesse. It is not forcefully applied; it's implied. Hospitalitarians are not offensive, but we might invite and cajole you to join us; we open new doors for people. We are the door-minders to a unique experience. We invite you to come and play. That's the tribe I want to belong to.

I see the members of this tribe among us every day, each in their own free-form dance. It is a graceful dance with humanity. It is about focusing on values rather than objectives. We don't sell, we invite. It's membership through osmosis. It is the presenting of the lei. A lei that is given freely, with intent. A lei that is perpetually abundant.

We move to this state through conscious preparation. Like your muscles, stretching increases agility, which increases strength that opens us to opportunities that we could have never performed before. As these opportunities present themselves, we embrace them effortlessly, gracefully, because through practice, we have become more limber, stronger. Like great athletes, we have taken our discipline seriously, and with practice, we make it look easy and fun. We take our discipline seriously, but we don't take ourselves seriously. We are humble. Hospitality is the balance of discipline and beauty. It is receiving others in a grace that lives deep in the soul.

This takes courage. Courage to let things go and move past paralyzing situations. It's life Aikido, using potentially adverse energy to benefit a connection. We face it and move through it. Instead of resistance or countering the energy, we change it. We redirect, and the energy is not diminished but transformed. The energy becomes useful to both you and others.

As hospitalitarians, we each get more out of hospitality than we put into it. It does not deplete; it recharges. You are not giving yourself as a martyr; you are recharging yourself because you know who you truly are. It comes from a place of strength. And with this strength, you are growing every day, nurturing yourself and allowing yourself to grow in your own way, an individual with a purposeful, joyous life.

It is a life based on trust. When we learn to trust ourselves and others, we become surrounded by trust. Trust is the endgame for each of us and our business. Trust has truth at its core. Truth is the building block of trust. Without truth, trust falls apart. Without trust, relationships are strained, businesses have difficulty thriving, and we find it burdensome to grow as human beings. Trust is that important. Trusting yourself is most important.

Toward the end of my talk with Talulah and Ruby, I told them a little about the book that I was writing, including my working title at the time, "Hospitality Quest." They both approved of the idea, and Ruby added thoughtfully, "I really love that name because you are really trying to find the hospitality in you and the kindness." Yes I am, Ruby. Yes, I am.

Not the end.

Acknowledgments

THIS BOOK WOULD NEVER have been possible without the love, openness, and freedom offered by my parents, Adrian and Jean Heintz. They set the tone; I merely took it from there. Also thank you to my great friend David O'Malley, my frequent sounding board, perpetual safety net, and consistent companion.

I would like to thank all the hospitality practitioners whose examples have inspired and kept the light of graciousness alive in me, including: Richie Rosen, Jen Garris, Annie and Craig Stoll, Tony Abou-Ganim, Julio Bermejo, Lorenza Trejo Lerdo, Glenn and Pam Hugo, David (Cheese) McNees, Sally Srok, Chuck Wagner, Charlie Wagner, Jenny Wagner Clark, Curtis and Jessica DeFede, Frank Altamura, Tim Bodell, Tim Hanni, Will Simkins, Rich Wood, John (JR) Rossetti, Don Wetherell, Monica Reilly, Dave Zepf, Danny Sam, Trish Tracey, Marco Wright, Maureen Donegan, Pete Sittnick, Richard Miyashiro, Aubrey Bailey, Taylor Kindred, Bettina Rouas, Staffan Terje, Jason Denton, Giovanni Scala, Doug Washington, John Cunin, Bill Higgins, Doug Beiderbecke, Jeremiah Tower, Greg Leadley, Byran McWaters, Mick Salyer, and the hospitality practitioners who have passed: Donna Scala, Luigi Marateo, Manny Goodman, Manny Heller, Harry Denton, Howard Lane, and Brian "King of the BDF" Johnson.

And thank you to my professional helpers: Julia Allen, Katie McKay, Caroline Laughlin, Jessica Reyes, Kimberly Lance, Pam Nordberg,

Nick Stegall, Jay Hodges, Daniel Sandoval, Mary Samson, Amanda Marquette, Tiffany Barrientos, and all of the people working behind the scenes at Greenleaf Book Group.

We can't end the thank-yous without mentioning the authors that inspired this book: Danny Meyer, don Miguel Ruiz, Eckhart Tolle, Rosa Say, Neale Donald Walsch, and of course Lao Tzu.

Notes

CHAPTER 1

1. Danny Meyer, *Setting the Table: The Transforming Power of Hospitality in Business* (New York: HarperCollins, 2006).

CHAPTER 2

1. Bruce Springsteen, *Born to Run* (Newark: Audible, 2016).

2. Harry Coverte, "Side Dish," *SF Weekly*, 4/21/1999, https://www.sfweekly.com/dining/side-dish-29/.

3. Eckhart Tolle, *The Power of Now* (Novato, CA: New World Library, 1999), 14.

4. Don Miguel Ruiz, *The Four Agreements* (San Rafael, CA: Amber-Allen Publishing, 2018), 28.

5. Ruiz, *Four Agreements*, 32.

6. Ruiz, *Four Agreements*, 43.

7. Neale Donald Walsch, *Conversations with God, Book 3* (Charlottesville, VA: Hampton Roads Publishing, 2020), 357.

8. Sir Arthur Conan Doyle, *The Sign of the Four* (Sea Wolf Press, 2019), 37.

CHAPTER 3

1. Tolle, *Power of Now*, 24.

2. Tolle, *Power of Now*, 27.

3. Paul Pearsall, *The Pleasure Prescription: To Love, to Work, to Play—Life in the Balance* (Alameda, CA: Hunter House Inc. Publishers, 1996), 85–86.

4. Seth Godin, *Tribes* (New York: Portfolio, 2008), 11.

CHAPTER 4

1. Mary Kawena Pukui, E.W. Haertig M.D., Catherine A. Lee, *Nānā I Ke Kumu: Look to the Source*, Volume 1 (Honolulu, Hawaii: Hui Hanai, 1983), 119.

2. Lawrence H. Fuchs, *Hawaiian Pono: A Social History. The 50th State, Its People and Politics from Annexation to Statehood* (New York: Harcourt, Brace & World, Inc., 1961), 74.

3. Rosa Say, *Managing with Aloha: Bringing Hawaii's Universal Values to the Art of Business* (Waikoloa, Hawaii: Ho'ohana Publishing, 2004), 241.

4. Say, *Managing with Aloha*, 27.

5. Say, *Managing with Aloha*, 28.

6. Say, *Managing with Aloha*, 21.

7. Pila of Hawaii, *The Secrets and Mysteries of Hawaii* (Deerfield Beach, Florida: Health Communications Inc., 1995), 222.

8. Pukui, Haertig, Lee, *Nānā I Ke Kumu*, Volume 1, 43.

9. Pukui, Haertig, Lee, *Nānā I Ke Kumu*, 40.

10. Pukui, Haertig, Lee, *Nānā I Ke Kumu*, 118–119.

11. Pukui, Haertig, Lee, *Nānā I Ke Kumu*, 119.

12. Rosa Say, *Managing with Aloha: Bringing Hawaii's Universal Values to the Art of Business* (Waikoloa, Hawaii: Ho'ohana Publishing, 2004), 241.

13. John (Fire) Lame Deer, Richard Erdoes, *Lame Deer, Seeker of Visions* (New York: Simon & Schuster Paperbacks, 2009), 70–71.

14. Henri J. M. Nouwen, *Reaching Out: The Three Movements of the Spiritual Life* (New York: Doubleday, 1975), 68.

15. Parker J. Palmer, *The Courage to Teach: Exploring the Inner Landscape of a Teacher's Life* (San Francisco: Jossey-Bass, 2017), 51.

16. Lao Tzu, *Tao Te Ching*, translated by John C. H. Wu (Boulder, CO: Shambala Publications, 2006), 151.

17. Lao Tzu, *Tao Te Ching*, 151.

18. Danny Meyer, *Setting the Table: The Transforming Power of Hospitality in Business* (New York: HarperCollins, 2006).

19. Meyer, *Setting the Table*, 238.

CHAPTER 5

1. Neale Donald Walsch, *Conversations with God, Book 3* (Charlottesville, VA: Hampton Roads Publishing, 2020), 357.

CHAPTER 7

1. Lonni Collins Pratt, Daniel Homan, *Radical Hospitality: Benedict's Way of Love.* (Brewster, MA: Paraclete Press, 2011), 74.

About the Author

ORN IN THE MIDWEST, Eddie Heintz fell in love with the great outdoors and bartending in equal measure. Moving to San Francisco in 1985, he established himself in "The City's" restaurants as an effective fly-by-the-seat-of-your-pants manager. After more than a decade managing some of San Francisco's top restaurants he began to grow restless. An opportunity on the Big Island of Hawaii enabled him to practice and fine-tune his passion: embracing great hospitality as a lifestyle. Four years later and armed with the spirit of Aloha, he returned to the mainland, where he engaged with staff and guests in restaurants, resorts, wineries, and as an instructor at the Culinary Institute of America at Greystone. He is currently practicing his style of hospitality in Napa, California.

Made in United States
Orlando, FL
01 February 2022

14292947R10104